THE WI BOOK
— OF —
VEGETARIAN CUISINE

SIAN COOK

WI BOOKS

Copyright © National Federation of Women's Institutes
First Published 1999 by WI Books

in association with Stable Ltd
Glebe House, Church Street,
Crediton, Devon EX17 2AF
Illustrated by Michael Lye

British Library Cataloguing in Publication Data.
A CIP catalogue record for this book is available from the British Library.

ISBN 0 947990 67 4

Printed and bound in Great Britain by Short Run Press Ltd, Exeter, Devon

Acknowledgements

I would like to thank my husband, Terry, for his endless patience in unscrambling all the work on his computer – apparently I kept filing the recipes in strange places! I would also like to thank him and our two daughters, Holly and Amy (who would have them in puréed form), for having to taste a wide variety of dishes. Holly would often say, "Oh, no, not another taster!"

CONTENTS

CONTENTS

CONTENTS

INTRODUCTION

Vegetarian cooking has undergone a huge transformation in recent years. When I first became a vegetarian, about fifteen years ago, it was difficult to eat imaginative and interesting food: at home, at dinner parties and in restaurants. There were a number of reasons for this: there wasn't the range of foods available all year round in the supermarkets as there is now, vegetarian cookbooks were few and far between, chefs were not experienced in creating imaginative dishes and, lastly, people assumed that you only ate wholefoods, so everything was brown and heavy.

Fortunately, things have improved since those days. However, vegetarians still only have the option of dishes such as vegetarian lasagne / chilli / curry or mushroom Stroganoff when they eat out in restaurants or in people's homes, as many people do not have the confidence or ability to cook anything more adventurous. I remember being thrilled when my husband took me to a restaurant called Inigo Jones in Covent Garden about ten years ago and I was presented with a special Vegetarian Menu – this was unheard of then, and even these days a Vegetarian is lucky if he or she is offered a choice.

The purpose of this book is to provide you with a wide range of recipes that are suitable for special eating occasions when so often vegetarians feel they are the 'poor relation'. These occasions are entertaining friends at formal dinner parties or informal lunches or suppers; Christmas, when in the past vegetarians were only ever offered a nut roast; and also barbeques, when the choice was usually vegetarian sausages or burgers, or a jacket potato.

Some vegetarians like to eat meat-substitute meals. By and large I do not, although one exception for me is a product called Quorn, which is a micro-protein and is the ultimate healthy food as it is high in protein and fibre and low in fat. It should be treated much as you would treat cooked chicken. I like it because of its texture and the fact that it has very little taste, so it will absorb any flavours you add to your chosen dish.

Mushrooms and aubergines also add a firm texture to a dish and are therefore ideal replacements for meat in recipes. I feel strongly that recipes should only be used as guidelines MOST of the time, so that the cook can adapt the ingredients to suit their preferences as well as availability. I apologise for the number of recipes that contain these two ingredients – I just love them!

Strict vegetarians do not use gelatine. Many products, such as ice cream, contain gelatine that you would not suspect unless you read all packs carefully. There are alternatives available such as Vege-gel and gelazone but I don't find they work as well as gelatine. Please use whichever you feel happiest using but you will need to follow the pack instructions carefully.

Quite often you will find that you are catering for vegetarians and meat-eaters at the same time. Some of my recipes, particularly the main course ones, give suggestions for adapting them for meat-eaters, where it is practical to do so.

I hope that you have great pleasure in cooking and eating these recipes and that the book takes away the worry and fear from creating delicious and imaginative vegetarian food for special occasions. Don't be afraid to cheat; for example, if a recipe includes a tomato or cheese sauce, just buy a good ready-made one if it makes your life easy!

STARTERS

CHILLI BEAN AND PEPPER SOUP

Serves 6

A colourful soup with a kick which is delicious served with an AVOCADO SALSA (page 70) – the salsa adds texture and contrasting colour, as well as acting as a cooler!

30 ml (2 tbsp) sunflower oil
1 large onion, finely chopped
4 garlic cloves, peeled
   and finely chopped
2 red peppers, de-seeded
   and finely chopped
2 red chillies, de-seeded
   and finely chopped
1 litre (1³/₄ pints) vegetable stock
850 ml (1¹/₂) pints passata

30 ml (2 tbsp) tomato purée
15 ml (1 tbsp) sun-dried tomato purée
30 ml (2 tbsp) sweet chilli sauce
395 g (14 oz) can red kidney beans
45 g (1¹/₂ oz) tortilla crisps, crushed
30 ml (2 tbsp) fresh coriander, finely
   chopped
140 ml (¹/₄ pint) sour cream
fresh coriander, to garnish

1. Heat the oil in a large saucepan and fry the onion and garlic until soft, taking care not to brown. Stir in the peppers and chillies and fry for a few minutes. Stir in the remaining ingredients, except the last two and bring to the boil. Cover and simmer for half an hour.

2. Allow to cool a little and then process until smooth. Return to the saucepan and bring to the boil. Remove from the heat, stir in the sour cream and check the seasoning. Serve in bowls garnished with coriander and with some AVOCADO SALSA (page 70).

COURGETTE AND FETA SOUP

Serves 4–6

This is a delicious soup and simple to make. It freezes readily and can therefore be prepared well in advance. Blue Brie can be substituted for the feta cheese, if wished.

30 ml (2 tbsp) olive oil
1 large onion, peeled and diced
2 cloves garlic, peeled and crushed
3 large or 4 medium courgettes,
    cut into slices

1 large potato, peeled and diced
2.5 ml ($\frac{1}{2}$ tsp) each dried thyme / parsley
710 ml ($1\frac{1}{4}$ pints) good vegetable stock
salt and fresh ground black pepper
85 g (3 oz) feta cheese, in small pieces

1. Fry the onion and garlic in the oil for a few minutes until softened. Add the courgettes and potato and sauté gently for 10 mins. Add the herbs, stock, a little salt (feta is a salty cheese), and pepper, bring to the boil and then simmer gently, covered, for 20 mins until the vegetables are very tender.
2. Process the soup in a blender or liquidiser until completely smooth. Stir in the feta cheese and stir until melted. Check the seasoning and serve with some warm crusty bread.

ROAST ROOT VEGETABLE SOUP

Serves 6

Roasting the vegetables is well worth the effort – it gives the soup an extra depth of flavour. Do vary the vegetables according to your taste and their availability.

1 celeriac, peeled
1 large parsnip, peeled
2 carrots, peeled
1 onion, skinned
1 large sweet potato, peeled
45 ml (3 tbsp) olive oil

15 ml (1 tbsp) finely chopped fresh parsley
15 ml (1 tbsp) fresh thyme leaves
sea salt and fresh ground black pepper
850 ml ($1\frac{1}{2}$) pints good vegetable stock
single cream, to serve

1. Cut the vegetables into evenly-sized pieces. Place in a roasting tin in one layer, cover with oil and sprinkle with herbs. Season well and toss to ensure that all the vegetables are coated in oil and herbs. Marinate for at least half an hour.
2. Pre-heat the oven to 230°C, 445°F, Gas 8. Roast the vegetables for $\frac{3}{4}$ hour until they are tinged brown and are nearly cooked. Transfer to a large saucepan, add the stock, bring to the boil and simmer, covered, for 15 mins until the vegetables are very tender.
3. Blend the vegetables and stock in a liquidiser or food processor until completely smooth. Check the seasoning. Pour into bowls and add swirls of cream.

ROAST PEPPER MOUSSE

Serves 6

I love recipes which have just a handful of ingredients, are straightforward to make and have a depth of flavour that gives the impression that a lot of time has been spent creating it. You could substitute feta cheese for the cream cheese but no salt will need to be added as feta is salty.

450 g (1 lb) peppers,
   quartered and de-seeded
225 g (8 oz) Greek yoghurt
200 g (7 oz) cream cheese

1 sachet gelatine or 15 ml (3 tsp)
   vegetarian equivalent
5 ml (1 tsp) balsamic vinegar
salt and ground pepper

1. Heat the grill, and grill the peppers until the skins blister and blacken. Put in a plastic bag to cool – the skins will loosen. Skin and roughly chop the flesh.
2. Sprinkle the gelatine over 45ml (3 tbsp) cold water in a bowl and dissolve by stirring over a pan of hot water or heating in the microwave for 30 seconds on high. Allow to cool. Process the peppers and gelatine and then add the yoghurt, cream cheese and vinegar. Season.
3. Lightly oil and line with cling film a 450 g (1 lb) loaf tin and spoon the mousse mixture into the tin. Place in the fridge to set.
4. Invert onto a plate, remove the cling film and cut into thick slices. Serve with a seasonal salad tossed in a balsamic vinaigrette.

CAULIFLOWER AND BROCCOLI LOAF WITH TOMATO VINAIGRETTE

Serves 8

This is a versatile recipe: as well as a starter, it could be served as the vegetable accompaniment to a main course or as part of a buffet as it looks so impressive.

340 g (12 oz) broccoli florets
340 g (12 oz) cauliflower florets
200 g (7 oz) cream cheese or Boursin
2 eggs, lightly beaten
   in two separate bowls
115 g (4 oz) mature Cheddar, grated
salt and fresh ground black pepper
15 ml (1 tbsp) olive oil

1 onion, peeled and chopped
2 cloves garlic, peeled and crushed
2.5 ml ($\frac{1}{2}$ tsp) Dijon mustard
60 ml (4 tbsp) olive oil
15 ml (1 tbsp) red wine vinegar
6 ripe tomatoes, skinned,
   de-seeded and chopped
15 ml (1 tbsp) freshly snipped chives

1. Pre-heat the oven to 180°C, 355°F, Gas 4. Line and lightly oil a 1.1 litre (2 pint) loaf tin.

2. Cook the broccoli and cauliflower in separate saucepans until tender and drain. Meanwhile, fry the onion and garlic in the oil until the onion is soft. Blend the broccoli with half the cream cheese, one egg, half the cheese and half the onions and season well. Repeat with the cauliflower. Spoon the broccoli mixture into the prepared tin and level the surface and top with the cauliflower mixture. Cover with a piece of oiled foil. Put in a roasting tin, half fill with hot water and bake for 45–50 mins until firm to the touch. Leave to cool.

3. To make the dressing, whisk together the mustard, oil and vinegar. Season and then add the tomatoes and chives.

4. To serve, turn out the terrine, cut into slices and serve with a little dressing and garnish with some salad leaves.

CREAMY CARROT AND ORANGE PATE

Serves 6–8

This paté is universally popular and is also a great way to get children to eat a very healthy vegetable dish! Try and use organic carrots as the flavour is far superior. The paté freezes very well – it is best to thaw it overnight in the fridge.

225 g (8 oz) carrots, peeled and sliced
140 ml ($^{1}/_{4}$ pint) fresh orange juice
55 g (2 oz) fresh wholemeal breadcrumbs
30 g (1 oz) dried apricots, finely chopped
30 g (1 oz) sultanas
225 g (8 oz) cream cheese
3 large eggs, lightly beaten
15 ml (1 tbsp) freshly chopped coriander
salt and freshly ground black pepper

1. Grease and line a 450 g (1 lb) loaf tin with baking parchment. Place the carrots in a saucepan with the orange juice, bring to the boil and simmer very gently, covered, for about 15–20 mins until the carrots are soft.

2. Pre-heat the oven to 180°C, 355°F, Gas 4. Blend the carrots with the breadcrumbs, cream cheese, eggs and coriander. Fold in the apricots and sultanas. Season well. Pour into prepared tin, level the surface. Fill a roasting tin with a good inch (2.5 cm) of hot water, place the loaf tin in the centre. Bake in the oven for 45–50 mins until firm. Take out of the roasting tin, allow to cool in the loaf tin.

3. Remove from the tin when cold by running a knife around the edges and inverting onto a plate. Cut into fairly thick slices, place onto serving plate. Garnish with a green salad and carrot curls (take thin strips off a carrot using a potato peeler and then immersing in iced water to 'set' the curls).

BAKED ITALIAN AUBERGINE SLICES

Serves 4

This versatile starter can be served at room temperature as part of a cold buffet or in a large gratin dish for two people for supper, with a salad and crusty bread.

1 large fat aubergine
salt and fresh ground black pepper
olive oil
1 medium onion, finely chopped
2 cloves garlic,
    peeled and finely chopped
15 ml (1 tbsp) fresh parsley, finely chopped

15 ml (1 tbsp) fresh thyme leaves
    or pinch dried thyme
395 g (14 oz) can chopped tomatoes
15 ml (1 tbsp) tomato purée
2.5 ml ($\frac{1}{2}$ tsp) sugar
70 g ($2\frac{1}{2}$ oz) Mozzarella cheese, diced
8 fresh basil leaves

1. Cut the aubergine into 8 thick discs. Reserve the ends for another dish. Place in a colander, sprinkle liberally with salt. Leave for an hour, rinse, then pat dry.
2. In the meantime, make the tomato sauce. Cook the onion, garlic, parsley and thyme gently in 30 ml (2 tbsp) olive oil until tender. Add the tomatoes, tomato purée and sugar, bring to the boil and cook over a high heat, stirring frequently until there is no trace of wateriness. Taste and adjust the seasoning.
3. Pre-heat the oven to 180°C, 355°F, Gas 4. Oil an oven-proof dish generously and lay the aubergine slices in a single layer, without overlapping. Brush lightly with olive oil. Cover with foil and bake for about $\frac{1}{2}$ hour until the aubergine is tender but still firm.
4. Uncover the aubergine and spread the slices thickly with the tomato sauce, making sure that the sauce does not go over the edges. Dot the Mozzarella pieces on top, then return to the oven for 15 mins.
5. Place two slices onto each plate and garnish each slice with a basil leaf.

FLORENTINE MUSHROOMS

Serves 4

I make no apologies for including two stuffed mushroom recipes. They are such a wonderful dish for a vegetarian at a special meal – visually appealing, full of flavour and can be assembled well in advance and then cooked just before eating.

4 large portabello mushrooms
20 ml (4 tsp) pesto
55 g (2 oz) goat's cheese
30 ml (2 tbsp) olive oil
1 small onion, peeled and finely diced
1 clove garlic, peeled and crushed

115 g (4 oz) frozen spinach, thawed
    pinch freshly grated nutmeg
4 sun-dried tomatoes, finely chopped
30 ml (2 tbsp) wholemeal breadcrumbs
30 ml (2 tbsp) freshly grated Parmesan
salt and freshly ground black pepper

1. Pre-heat the oven to 200ºC, 390ºF, Gas 6. Remove stalks from the mushrooms, chop finely and set aside. Brush the mushrooms all over with half the olive oil, place in a large shallow oven-proof dish, cover with foil and bake for 20 mins.
2. Fry the onion and garlic in the remaining oil for about 5 mins, without colour, until softened. Add the spinach and nutmeg. Cook until any liquid has evaporated. Stir in the sun-dried tomatoes. Season with salt and pepper.
3. Spread each mushroom cavity with a teaspoon of pesto, dot with small pieces of goat's cheese and top with the spinach mixture. Combine the bread-crumbs and Parmesan cheese and sprinkle over the spinach. Place, uncovered, in the oven and bake for about 15 mins until crisp and golden.
4. Serve hot with a salad garnish and crusty bread.

POLENTA PIZZAS   Serves 6

Polenta is made from corn or maize and can be like a mash when freshly made or becomes quite firm when allowed to cool and set. In this recipe, I have allowed the mixture to set so that it forms the base for mini pizzas. They make a very attractive starter to a dinner party (they can be prepared well in advance), or form part of a buffet. They can be baked on the barbeque or in a conventional oven.

105 ml (7 tbsp) butter
1 onion, peeled and finely chopped
250 g (9 oz) 'instant' polenta
1 litre (1³/₄ pints) water
salt and fresh ground black pepper
pinch crushed dried chillies

1 large long aubergine, discard
   the ends and cut into 6 slices
extra virgin olive oil
4 ripe tomatoes
pesto sauce
30 ml (2 tbsp) freshly grated Parmesan

1. Melt the butter in a large pan and fry the onion over a gentle heat until softened. Add the water and bring to the boil. Pour in the polenta in a thin and steady stream, stirring constantly. Return to the boil then reduce the heat and simmer very gently for 5 mins and continue to stir. Beat in the butter until it has melted and then stir in the salt, pepper and chillies. Pour the mixture onto a large, oiled baking sheet and leave to cool and set.
2. Brush both sides of the aubergine with olive oil and grill until golden brown and softened. Pre-heat the oven to 180ºC, 355ºF, Gas 4.
3. Using a 7.5 cm (3 ins) cutter, cut out 6 circles from the polenta. (Cut the rest into bite-sized pieces and deep-fry for a tasty snack.) Place on a baking sheet and spread each one with some pesto sauce. Arrange about 3 slices of tomato on top, then an aubergine slice, and sprinkle with the Parmesan cheese. Bake in the oven for 15–20 mins until cooked and the cheese is golden brown.

ROASTED RED PEPPER HOUMOUS

Serves 6

This is a variation on traditional houmous. Roasted red peppers add colour and flavour to this popular dip. As the peppers add moisture when blended, far less olive oil is needed than usual, making it less calorific!

3 large red peppers, halved and de-seeded
15 ml (1 tbsp) extra virgin olive oil
425 g (15 oz) can chickpeas, drained and rinsed
2 large cloves garlic, peeled and chopped
15 g ($^1/_2$ oz) fresh coriander, thick stalks removed
30 ml (2 tbsp) fresh lemon juice
salt and fresh ground black pepper

1. Place the peppers under a hot grill and cook until blackened. Place in a plastic bag and cool.
2. Blend with all the remaining ingredients and chill for a few hours, if possible, for the flavours to develop. Serve with hot pitta bread.

TWICE-BAKED MUSHROOM SOUFFLES

Serves 6–8

Twice-baked soufflés are wonderful for entertaining. They can be prepared in advance and returned to the oven as guests are given drinks at the table! It is worth using the dried mushrooms as they and their soaking liquid accentuate the mushroom flavour.

15 g ($^1/_2$ oz) dried porcini mushrooms
140 ml ($^1/_4$ pint) hot water
45 g (1$^1/_2$ oz) butter
170 g (6 oz) chestnut mushrooms, sliced
30 g (1 oz) plain flour

170 ml (6 fl oz) milk
85 g (3 oz) mature Cheddar cheese, grated
3 large eggs, separated
30–40 ml (6–8 tsp) freshly grated
   Parmesan cheese

1. Pre-heat the oven to 200°C, 390°F, Gas 6. Butter and base line 6–8 ramekin dishes. Pour the hot water over the DRIED mushrooms and leave to soak for 15–20 mins. Drain them well, reserving the stock and finely chop them.
2. Melt the butter and fry the chestnut mushrooms gently until softened. Drain 6–8 slices from the pan, reserve for garnishing the soufflés. Stir in the flour and cook for a couple of minutes, stirring all the time. Gradually whisk in the milk and mushroom stock and stir until thickened. Remove from the heat and stir in the reserved dried mushrooms, egg yolks and grated Cheddar. Whisk the egg whites until stiff and fold into the sauce carefully.

3. Spoon the mixture into the ramekins and bake in a roasting tin half-filled with hot water for 15–20 mins until risen and golden. Allow to cool. Reduce the oven temperature to 180°C, 355°F, Gas 4.

4. To serve, turn the soufflés out of their dishes, remove the paper from the bases and put them onto a greased baking sheet. Top each soufflé with a teaspoon of Parmesan cheese and bake for 15–20 mins until risen. Transfer to serving plates and garnish with the reserved mushroom slices and some salad leaves.

ROASTED CAPONATA BAKES   Serves 6

This is like a sweet and sour ratatouille. Roasting the vegetables is well worth the effort as the flavour is wonderful. Mozzarella or Brie can be substituted for the goat's cheese. Leftover caponata can be eaten cold in a salad or hot with vegetables.

90 ml (6 tbsp) extra virgin olive oil
75 ml (5 tbsp) red wine vinegar
45 ml (3 tbsp) soft brown sugar
45 ml (3 tbsp) tomato purée
1 large onion, peeled and roughly chopped
1 aubergine, cut into 2.5 cm (1 inch) dice
1 courgette, cut into 2.5 cm (1 inch) dice
2 sticks celery, cut into 1.25 cm ($^1/_2$ inch) lengths
225 g (8 oz) cherry tomatoes
4 sun-dried tomatoes, cut into tiny pieces
30 ml (2 tbsp) sultanas, soaked in hot water and drained
30 g (1 oz) pine kernels
140 g (5 oz) or 1$^1/_2$ logs of 100g (3$^1/_2$ oz) goat's cheese, cut into 6 equal slices

1. Pre-heat the oven to 200°C, 390°F, Gas 6. Whisk the olive oil with the vinegar, sugar and tomato purée in a large bowl, then add the onion, aubergine, courgette, celery, tomatoes and sun-dried tomatoes and toss well to make sure that all the vegetables are coated in the sauce.

2. Transfer to a roasting tin, spread evenly and season with salt and freshly ground black pepper. Roast for about 40 mins until the vegetables are soft and tinged brown at the edges. In the meantime, dry-fry the pine nuts until golden brown. When the vegetables are cooked, fold in the sultanas and pine nuts.

3. Spoon the caponata into 6 large ramekins, top with a slice of goat's cheese (cut side up when using the end slices) and return to the oven for 10–15 mins until the cheese is golden brown.

4. Serve with lots of crusty bread to mop up the lovely juices.

MUSHROOM, BEAN AND CORIANDER PATE   Serves 6–8

Do use chestnut mushrooms, as they have a more intense flavour than button mushrooms. Serve with salad leaves, including fresh coriander, and crusty bread.

1 onion, finely diced	340 g (12 oz) mushrooms, sliced
1 large clove garlic, peeled and crushed	395 g (14 oz) can cannellini beans, drained
55 g (2 oz) butter	250 g (9 oz) Ricotta cheese
5 ml (1 tsp) coriander, crushed	salt and fresh ground black pepper

1. Melt the butter and fry the onion and garlic gently for a few minutes until soft. Add the coriander seeds and fry for 30 seconds before adding the mushrooms. Continue to cook for 15 mins until the mushrooms are cooked and most of the liquid has evaporated. Cool a little and then blend the mushroom mixture with the beans and cheese, seasoning well.
2. Serve in individual ramekins, garnishing each with some coriander leaves.

COURGETTE MOULDS   Serves 6

The courgettes are grated to give a pretty, green speckled effect. Serve cold, garnished with salad leaves or warm, surrounded by sieved SUN-DRIED TOMATO SAUCE (page 70).

1 medium onion, finely chopped	285 ml (½ pint) milk
1 clove garlic, peeled and crushed	2 large eggs, lightly beaten
30 g (1 oz) butter	55 g (2 oz) Gruyère cheese, grated
30 g (1 oz) plain flour	salt and fresh ground black pepper
340 g (12 oz) courgettes, grated	

1. Pre-heat the oven to 180°C, 355°F, Gas 4. Grease and base line 6 ramekin dishes with baking parchment circles.
2. Melt the butter in a saucepan and fry the onion and garlic over a low heat until the onion has softened. Add the courgettes and stir well so that they are coated evenly in the garlic onions. Cook for a couple of minutes to soften. Sprinkle on the flour, mix well and cook for one minute. Gradually stir in the milk and bring to the boil. Allow to simmer for a further 2 mins, stirring from time to time. Remove from the heat and add the cheese. Season. Stir in the eggs thoroughly.
3. Spoon into the prepared ramekins, place in a roasting tin and add hot water to come up half the sides of the ramekins. Bake in the oven for 25–30 mins until they are risen slightly and are firm to the touch.

LIGHT LUNCHES AND SNACKS

MUSHROOMS IN A HOUMOUS SAUCE

Serves 4

This dish is simplicity itself and gives guests the impression that you have spent ages preparing it. It would make a delicious pasta supper by serving the sauce with tagliatelle or spaghetti and sprinkling with Parmesan cheese. You may wish to thin the sauce with a little milk or cream.

30 ml (2 tbsp) olive oil
1 small onion, peeled
   and finely chopped
225 g (8 oz) button mushrooms,
   sliced fairly thick

2.5 ml ($\frac{1}{2}$ tsp) cumin seeds (optional)
170 g (6 oz) houmous
20 ml (4 tsp) freshly grated Parmesan
salt and fresh ground black pepper

1. Fry the onion and cumin seeds, if using, in the olive oil over a low heat for a few minutes to soften, without browning.
2. Add the mushrooms and fry for a further 2–3 mins, stirring occasionally.
3. Stir in the houmous and cook until heated through. Check the seasoning.
4. Lightly oil 4 ramekins and spoon the mixture into the dishes. Sprinkle over the cheese.
5. Bake in the oven, pre-heated to 180°C, 355°F, Gas 4 for 15–20 mins, until the cheese has melted and the mushrooms are hot.
6. Serve with a side salad and fresh bread.

MINTED CUCUMBER CHEESE RING

Serves 6

This is a delicious summer starter or makes an attractive dish for a buffet. All you need to garnish it is sprigs of fresh watercress placed in the centre 'hole'. You can serve it in ramekins if the thought of turning out a mould frightens you!

½ large cucumber, coarsely grated
1 sachet gelatine or 15 ml (3 tsp) veg. equiv.
225g (8 oz) cream cheese
½ lemon, grated rind only

5 ml (1 tsp) mint sauce
285 ml (½ pint) soured cream
1 clove garlic, peeled and crushed
salt and ground black pepper

1. Put the cucumber in a piece of muslin or clean cloth and squeeze to remove most of the moisture. Dissolve the gelatine in 45 ml (3 tbsp) cold water by stirring over a pan of hot water or by heating in a microwave for 30 seconds. Allow to cool. Soften the cheese and stir in the cucumber, the lemon rind, mint sauce, soured cream, garlic and season with salt and pepper. Stir in the gelatine when it is the same temperature as the cheese mixture, making sure it is well blended.

2. Spoon into a wetted ring mould and chill for about 4 hours or until set. To serve, dip briefly into a bowl of hot water to loosen the sides and then invert onto a serving plate. Decorate with a bunch of watercress.

ITALIAN TOWERS

Serves 4

These towers look impressive but are easy to prepare in advance.

1 medium aubergine, trim the ends and cut into 8 slices
2 medium courgettes, trim the ends and the outside 'ends'
    and cut into thin strips lengthways
2 large beefsteak tomatoes, trim the top and bottom
    and cut each into 2 thick slices
115 g (4 oz) Mozzarella, siced into four
pesto sauce
salt and fresh ground black pepper
extra virgin olive oil
Parmesan cheese

1. Pre-heat the oven to 180°C, 355°F, Gas 4. Heat a little oil in a frying pan (preferably a griddle pan so that the aubergine and courgette slices have line marks) and fry the aubergine and courgette slices on both sides for a few minutes until they are golden brown and soft.

2. Lightly oil 4 large ramekin dishes. Place 2 pieces of courgette crossways in each dish with the ends slightly overlapping the rims. Spread a little pesto on one side of each aubergine slice and season with salt and pepper. Place one slice in each ramekin, pesto side up, add a slice of tomato, then Mozzarella, followed by the second aubergine slice, pesto side down. Place the courgette ends over the aubergine surface.
3. Place in the oven to warm through for 10 mins. To serve, invert onto serving plates, surround with tossed salad leaves which include some rocket. Make some Parmesan shavings by pulling a potato peeler along the edge of a piece of Parmesan cheese. Sprinkle these over the salad leaves.

AUBERGINE AND RED PEPPER CUSTARD FLAN   Serves 8

This flan conjures up everything that's Mediterranean. Liquidising the red peppers with the eggs, cream and milk gives the custard an attractive colour and complements the aubergine beautifully. I would serve it with a tossed green salad and some ciabatta bread.

225 g (8 oz) shortcrust pastry
1 long aubergine, cut into thin slices
30 ml (2 tbsp) olive oil
2 red peppers, quartered and de-seeded
4 large eggs

285 ml ($^1/_2$ pint) single cream
285 ml ($^1/_2$ pint) milk
salt and fresh ground black pepper
30 ml (2 tbsp) freshly grated Parmesan

1. Grill the peppers until the skin is turning black and is blistering. Put the peppers into a plastic bag to cool and loosen the skins (this can be done well in advance).
2. Pre-heat the oven to 190°C, 375°F, Gas 5. Place the aubergine slices on a greased baking sheet. Brush the surfaces lightly with olive oil, cover with foil and bake in the oven for 15–20 mins until the aubergine is cooked (the slices will be very pliable). Set to one side.
3. Roll out the pastry and line a 30.5 cm (12 ins) flan tin with the pastry. Prick the base, line with a sheet of foil or baking parchment and fill with baking beans. Cook for 10 mins, remove the foil/parchment and beans and return to the oven for a further 10 mins.
4. Skin the peppers and liquidise them with the eggs, cream, milk and seasoning. Arrange the aubergine slices, overlapping slightly, on the pastry base and then carefully pour in the pepper custard. Sprinkle the cheese on top and bake in the oven for 25–30 mins until the custard is set and the surface golden brown.

TOMATO AND MOZZARELLA SAUCE WITH PENNE

Serves 4

This delicious Italian tomato sauce is served with penne as the holes in the pasta will hold the sauce. A rocket salad with Parmesan curls go very well with this dish.

15 ml (1 tbsp) olive oil
1 onion, finely chopped
1 large clove garlic,
    peeled and crushed
2 celery sticks, finely chopped
395 g (14 oz) can chopped tomatoes
1 small red pepper, de-seeded and diced

285 ml (^{1}/$_2$ pint) vegetable stock
5 ml (1 tsp) pesto sauce
5 ml (1 tsp) sugar
225 g (8 oz) Mozzarella cheese, cubed
55 g (2 oz) pitted black olives, quartered
salt and fresh ground black pepper
225 g (8 oz) penne

1. Fry the onion, garlic and celery in the oil for a few minutes, to soften. Add the tomatoes, red pepper, stock, pesto sauce and sugar. Bring to the boil, cover and simmer for 30 mins, stirring from time to time. Purée half the mixture and return to the other half. Season and add the olives and Mozzarella and re-heat until the cheese is beginning to melt.
2. Cook the pasta according to the pack instructions, drain well and add to the sauce. Toss well before serving.

TOMATO AND GOAT'S CHEESE FRITTATA

Serves 6

This is like a quiche without the pastry – ideal to serve for a light lunch or supper and is ideal for picnics as it transports so well. It is best served warm or at room temperature accompanied by a dressed salad and some crusty Italian bread.

1 onion, peeled and sliced thinly
30 ml (2 tbsp) extra virgin olive oil
2 cloves garlic, peeled and crushed
1 courgette, trimmed and cut
    into medium slices
3 ripe tomatoes, peeled, de-seeded
    and chopped

3 sun-dried tomatoes, chopped (optional)
salt and fresh ground black pepper
30 g (1oz) butter
6 large eggs, lightly beaten
100 g (3^1/$_2$ oz) firm goat's cheese,
    cut into 6 discs

1. Fry the onion and garlic in the olive oil over a very gentle heat for about 10 mins by which time the onion will be tinged brown.
2. Add the courgette slices and cook for a few more minutes on both sides. Add the tomatoes and cook for a couple of minutes. Season well and then spoon onto absorbent paper.
3. Wash the frying pan and then melt the butter in it over a very low heat. Combine the eggs and vegetables in a large bowl and then pour into the frying pan. Cook the frittata very gently until it is set and golden underneath.
4. Just before it has reached this stage, heat the grill and place the goat's cheese discs in a circle on top of the frittata.
5. Place the pan under the grill for a couple of minutes until the top has set and the cheese is beginning to melt. Slide it onto a serving plate.

BLUE BRIE AND RED PEPPER CHEESECAKE   Serves 8–10

I created this recipe a number of years ago and I still have pleasure in making it – it is always popular. It can be served as a starter, as a light lunch with a salad and crusty bread or as part of a buffet.

85 g (3 oz) butter, melted
85 g (3 oz) wholemeal biscuits, crushed
55 g (2 oz) chopped and toasted hazelnuts
salt and fresh ground black pepper
1 sachet gelatine or 15 ml (3 tsp) vegetarian equivalent
60 ml (4 tbsp) water
115 g (4 oz) (after rind has been removed) Blue Brie
225 g (8 oz) curd cheese
285 ml ($^{1}/_{2}$ pint) Greek yoghurt
$^{1}/_{2}$ red pepper, de-seeded and finely chopped
red pepper 'diamonds', whipped cream and paprika, to decorate

1. Lightly oil a 20.5 cm (8 ins) cheesecake tin. Combine the first four ingredients to make the base. Press into the tin (I use a potato masher) and put into the fridge to set while making the filling.
2. Dissolve the gelatine or vegetarian equivalent in the water over a pan of hot water and allow to cool.
3. Beat together the cheeses and yoghurt, stir in the dissolved setting agent thoroughly and season well. Fold in the pepper pieces and then spoon the mixture onto the base. Chill until set. Decorate by sprinkling with paprika and swirls of cream topped with the pepper 'diamonds'.

DOUBLE GOAT'S CHEESE SALAD

Serves 4

This is a must for all lovers of goat's cheese. It can be made more substantial by serving the cheese halves on croutes.

2 x 100 g (2 x 3½ oz) Somerset goat's cheese (the completely rind-covered sort)
packet salad leaves (rocket salad is ideal)
cherry tomatoes
10 ml (2 tsp) lemon juice
5 ml (1 tsp) Dijon mustard
200 g (7 oz) Greek yoghurt
45 g (1½ oz) soft goat's cheese
salt and fresh ground black pepper
pine nuts, toasted (optional)

1. First of all, make the dressing by blending the lemon juice, mustard, yoghurt and soft goat's cheese thoroughly. Season with salt and pepper.
2. Pre-heat the grill. Slice each goat's cheese in half and place under the grill, cut side upwards. Grill until the surfaces are brown and the cheese is melting.
3. While they are cooking, arrange the salad leaves on serving plates and place some tomatoes on the leaves. Just before the cheese is ready, spoon the dressing onto the salad leaves. Sprinkle with the pine nuts, if using.

PEAR, SPINACH AND ARTICHOKE SALAD

Serves 4–6

This is a very pretty salad and full of contrasting flavours. It's also extremely healthy. If you are watching your calories, you could use half-fat crème fraiche and halve the amount of blue cheese used.

115 ml (4 fl oz) crème fraiche
115 g (4 oz) blue cheese
2 ripe avocado pears
2 ripe pears
juice 1 lemon
395 g (14 oz) can artichoke hearts
225 g (8 oz) baby spinach leaves
salt and fresh ground black pepper

1. Melt the blue cheese in the crème fraiche in a saucepan over a very gentle heat and then leave it to cool.
2. Peel and chop both varieties of pears and dip in the lemon juice to prevent discolouration. Drain and chop the artichoke hearts and mix in with the pears. Season with salt and pepper.
3. Arrange the spinach leaves on a serving platter or individual serving plates. Spoon the pear and artichoke mixture in the centre of the plate(s). Drizzle some of the dressing over the salad and then spoon the rest of the dressing into a small bowl to put on the side so that guests can help themselves to more.

MOROCCAN COUSCOUS SALAD

Serves 4–6

I like to serve this salad on a hot summer's day. Sun-dried tomato bread goes well with it. If you have a large circular platter, arrange the roasted vegetables in the centre, surround with the couscous and then finally the salad leaves on the outside. Served this way, it would make a stunning centre-piece for a buffet.

1 large aubergine, cut into 2.5 cm (1 inch) chunks
2 medium courgettes, cut into thick slices
1 red onion, peeled and cut into 2.5 cm (1 inch) cubes
130 g (4¹/₂ oz) chestnut mushrooms, halved or whole, depending on size
1 red pepper, de-seeded and cut into 2.5cm (1 inch) cubes
4 firm ripe tomatoes, quartered
1 red chilli, de-seeded and finely chopped
45 ml (3 tbsp) extra virgin olive oil
2 cloves garlic, peeled and finely chopped
¹/₂ quantity HARISSA sauce (page 70)
170 g (6 oz) couscous
285 ml (¹/₂ pint) hot water or light vegetable stock
salt and fresh ground black pepper
packet salad leaves, e.g. herb or rocket

1. Pre-heat the oven to 240°C, 465°F, Gas 9.
2. Arrange the first seven ingredients in a single layer in a large roasting tin then drizzle over the oil and sprinkle over the garlic. Season well with the salt and pepper. Mix thoroughly to ensure that all the vegetables are coated in the oil and garlic. Roast in the oven for about 30 mins until the vegetables are cooked and tinged brown on the edges. Remove from the oven and leave to cool.
3. Make the couscous by pouring the water or stock over the couscous in a large bowl and set aside for 5 mins or so, by which time all the liquid will have been absorbed. Stir it thoroughly with a fork. Add three teaspoons of the harissa and mix thoroughly.
4. Arrange the salad either as suggested above or in your chosen style and serve the remaining harissa separately.

BROCCOLI IN A BLUE CHEESE SAUCE

Serves 4

This is a variation on cauliflower cheese – broccoli replaces cauliflower and blue cheese the Cheddar cheese.

680 g (1¹/₂ lb) broccoli florets
55 g (2 oz) butter
55 g (2 oz) flour
570 ml (1 pint) milk

115 g (4 oz) blue cheese, e.g. Stilton
5 ml (1 tsp) Dijon mustard
salt and fresh ground black pepper

1. Pre-heat the oven to 180°C, 355°F, Gas 4. Cook the broccoli in boiling salted water until the florets are just tender.
2. Meanwhile, make the cheese sauce by whisking the butter, flour and milk together continuously over a moderate heat until it has thickened and reached boiling point. Lower the heat and simmer very gently for a couple of minutes to 'cook' the flour. Remove from the heat. Crumble in the blue cheese and stir until melted. Stir in the mustard and season with the salt and pepper.
3. Drain the broccoli and put in a gratin dish, pour over the sauce and bake in the oven for about 20 mins until the sauce is bubbling and golden brown.

WELSH RAREBIT SURPRISE

Serves 6

The 'surprise' is a layer of mango chutney under the cheese mixture. This is a 'fusion' recipe where ingredients from different cuisines are combined: in this case they are Welsh, Italian and Indian. It would make an unusual starter for a dinner party or it could be served for a light lunch with a watercress salad. It is delicious, either way!

1 ciabatta loaf, split in half
    horizontally and each half cut
    into 3 equal pieces
45 g (1¹/₂ oz) butter
340 g (12 oz) mature Caerphilly
    cheese, grated

75 ml (5 tbsp) beer or milk
pinch cayenne
7.5 ml (1¹/₂ tsp) mustard powder
3 egg yolks, lightly beaten
45 ml (3 tbsp) mango chutney
paprika

1. Pre-heat the oven to 200°C, 390°F, Gas 6. Melt the butter very gently in a saucepan which has a thick base. Add the cheese and stir until melted. Add the beer or milk very slowly, stirring all the time until smooth. Add the cayenne, mustard powder and egg yolks and stir to combine.

2. While making the cheese sauce, heat the bread through in the oven for a few minutes until it is slightly crusty. Pre-heat the grill. Spread the mango chutney on the cut surface and then top with the cheese mixture making sure that the chutney is hidden.
3. Place under the grill and cook until the cheese is golden brown. Sprinkle lightly with the paprika.

LEEK TERRINE WITH ROQUEFORT SAUCE   Serves 8

Leeks and Roquefort cheese have a natural affinity. Stilton or Danish Blue could be substituted for the Roquefort, as could broccoli for the leeks.

Terrine:
450 g (1 lb) leeks, thinly sliced
30 g (1 oz) butter or margerine
30 g (1 oz) plain flour
285 ml ($\frac{1}{2}$ pint) cold milk
140 g (5 oz) soft cheese with garlic and cheese, e.g. Boursin
3 large eggs
30 g (1 oz) fresh wholemeal breadcrumbs

Sauce:
30 g (1 oz) butter or margerine
140 ml ($\frac{1}{4}$ pint) dry white wine
285 ml ($\frac{1}{2}$ pint) vegetable stock
140 ml ($\frac{1}{4}$ pint) double cream
7.5 ml ($1\frac{1}{2}$ tsp) cornflour
70 g ($2\frac{1}{2}$ oz) Roquefort cheese

1. Pre-heat the oven to 180°C, 355°F, Gas 4.
2. Place the leeks in a saucepan of boiling water, lower the heat and simmer for about 5 mins until they are tender. Drain and rinse in cold water.
3. Make the sauce for the leeks by whisking butter, flour and milk over a moderate heat continuously until thick and starting to boil. Simmer for 2–3 mins.
4. Place the sauce in a blender with the leeks, cheese, eggs and breadcrumbs, and process until smooth. Season with salt and pepper.
5. Grease and line the base and short ends of a large loaf tin. Pour in the sauce and place into a roasting tin with enough hot water to come halfway up the tin.
6. Bake for 50–60 mins until firm and slightly risen. Stand for a few minutes before turning out. Allow to cool a little before slicing.
7. To make the Roquefort sauce, sauté the onion in the butter, which has been melted until soft. Add the wine and stock, bring to the boil and allow to boil until the liquid has been reduced by a half.
8. Strain through a sieve and return to the pan. Add the cream and bring to the boil. Whisk in the cream until it has melted. Season with a *little* salt (the Roquefort is salty) and fresh black pepper.
9. Place slices of the terrine on serving plates and pour the sauce around.

MAIN COURSES

PAPRIKA MUSHROOMS AND BUTTER BEANS   Serves 4

An interesting variation on mushroom Stroganoff. Try and use a variety of mushrooms – most supermarkets stock a wide variety,

30 g (1 oz) butter
15 ml (1 tbsp) olive oil
1 medium onion, finely chopped
2 cloves garlic, peeled and crushed
15 ml (1 tbsp) paprika
450 g (1 lb) mushrooms (e.g. button, chestnut, oyster and shitake)

5 ml (1 tsp) Dijon mustard
60 ml (4 tbsp) Sherry
425 g (15 oz) can butter beans, drained
10 ml (2 tsp) cornflour
30 ml (2 tbsp) finely chopped parsley
285 ml ($\frac{1}{2}$ pint) sour cream

1. Fry onion and garlic in the melted butter and oil until the onion is softened and slightly brown. Add the paprika and cook on a low heat for 3 mins.
2. Chop the mushrooms into even-sized pieces and add to the onions together with the butter beans and mustard and season with salt and fresh black pepper and cook over a gentle heat for about 5 mins until the mushrooms have softened.
3. Dissolve the cornflour in a little water. Add to the pan with the sherry and sour cream. Bring to the boil and simmer gently for a couple of minutes.
4. Serve with rice or pasta and sprinkle with a little finely chopped parsley.

BROCCOLI AND LENTIL BOLOGNESE BAKE   Serves 4

Here is a wholesome supper dish to serve at a winter supper party. A medley of carrots, peas and sweetcorn with plenty of crusty garlic bread would go perfectly with it.

170 g (6 oz) red lentils
5 ml (1 tsp) dried mixed herbs
1 large onion, peeled and chopped
30 ml (2 tbsp) olive oil
510 g (1 lb 2 oz) carton passata

30 ml (2 tbsp) tomato purée
5 ml (1 tsp) sugar
450 g (1 lb) broccoli florets
115 g (4 oz) Cheddar cheese, grated

1. Place the lentils in a pan with the herbs and plenty of water to cover. Bring to the boil and then simmer for about 15 mins until they are tender. Drain.
2. Fry the onion in the olive oil until softened. Add lentils, passata, tomato purée, sugar, salt and pepper. Bring to the boil, simmer for 15 mins. Check seasoning.
3. While the sauce is simmering, cook the broccoli, drain well and place in the bottom of a gratin dish. Pre-heat the grill. Spoon the sauce over the broccoli. Sprinkle the cheese on top. Grill until the cheese has melted and is golden brown.

SPINACH AND MOZZARELLA PEPPERS   Serves 4

These red peppers look so colourful filled with bright green spinach. You could serve one half as a starter or serve them as part of a buffet.

4 large red peppers
1 onion, finely chopped
2 cloves garlic, peeled and crushed
15 ml (1 tbsp) olive oil
425 g (15 oz) can chopped tomatoes
45 ml (3 tbsp) pesto sauce

250 g (9 oz) chopped frozen spinach,
   thawed and drained
45 ml (3 tbsp) pine nuts, toasted
115 g (4 oz) Mozzarella cheese, grated
15 ml (1 tbsp) freshly grated Parmesan
salt and fresh ground black pepper

1. Pre-heat the oven to 200°C, 390°F, Gas 6. Halve the peppers lengthways and remove the seeds. Place them in a saucepan, cover with water, bring to the boil, and simmer for about 8 mins. Meanwhile, fry the onion and garlic in the olive oil for a few minutes. Add the tomatoes, spinach and pesto sauce and cook over a gentle heat for a few minutes without a lid until most of the liquid has evaporated. Season well and fold in the pine nuts.
2. Place the peppers in a greased baking dish just large enough to hold them so that they fit in snugly. Fill with the spinach sauce, top with the Mozzarella and Parmesan cheeses. Bake for 30 mins until the cheeses are golden brown.

PARMIGIANA BAKE

Serves 4

Quorn gives the right texture to this Italian dish, traditionally made with chicken breast fillets. Black olives and mushrooms can be added, if wished. A tossed green salad and crusty Italian bread, such as ciabatta are ideal serving accompaniments.

340 g (12 oz) packet Quorn pieces
55 g (2 oz) Parmesan cheese,
   freshly grated
55 g (2 oz) plain flour
1 large egg, beaten lightly
30 g (1 oz) butter, melted
115 g (4 oz) Mozzarella cheese,
   sliced thinly

15 ml (1 tbsp) extra virgin olive oil
1 medium onion, chopped finely
1 large clove garlic, peeled and crushed
3 small courgettes, sliced fairly thickly
395 g (14 oz) can chopped tomatoes
15 ml (1 tbsp) sun-dried tomato purée
30 ml (2 tbsp) freshly chopped basil
salt and fresh black pepper

1. Pre-heat the oven to 180°C, 355°F, Gas 4.
2. Combine the flour with half of the Parmesan cheese. Dip the Quorn pieces in the beaten egg and then in the flour mixture.
3. Fry in the butter until golden brown and transfer to a gratin dish. Cover with Mozzarella. Wipe the frying pan with kitchen paper, add oil and gently fry the onion and garlic for a few minutes. Add courgettes and cook a further 2–3 mins.
4. Finally, add tomatoes, tomato purée, basil and seasoning. Simmer, uncovered, for 20 mins then spoon over the Quorn and Mozzarella. Cover loosely with foil and bake for 5 mins. Remove foil, sprinkle with remaining Parmesan and return to the oven for a further 10 mins until bubbling and golden brown.

Non-vegetarian tip: The Quorn could be replaced by cooked chicken pieces.

ROASTED VEGETABLE FAJITAS

Serves 6

The vegetables are given a bit of a 'kick' with the addition of some chillies and lime juice. Other vegetables can be substituted according to taste and availability.

2 red and 2 yellow peppers
3 courgettes
2 medium aubergines,
   cut into 2.5 cm (1 inch) cubes
170 g (6 oz) small button
   mushrooms, halved
90 ml (6 tbsp) olive oil

4 garlic cloves, chopped
30 ml (2 tbsp) chopped fresh herbs
   (e.g. thyme and rosemary)
1 lime, juice
2 red chillies (Anaheim), de-seeded
   and chopped
11.5 x 20.5 cm (4½ x 8 ins) flour tortillas

1. Place the vegetables in a large shallow dish. Combine the oil, garlic, herbs, lime juice and chillies and pour over the vegetables. Leave to marinate for a few hours, preferably overnight.
2. Pre-heat oven to 230°C, 445°F, Gas 8. Put vegetables and marinade into a large roasting tin. Roast for 25 mins, stirring occasionally, until charred and tender.
3. Warm the tortillas, fill with the vegetables, roll up and pour over the MEXICAN CHILLI SAUCE (page 68), sprinkle with grated Mozzarella, if wished, and serve with AVOCADO SALSA (page 70) and soured cream. If using the cheese, return the tortillas to the oven for a few minutes for the cheese to melt.

Non-vegetarian tip: You could stir-fry goujons or strips of turkey and add these to the roasted vegetables.

MEDITERRANEAN BAKE

Serves 4–6

This dish combines all the Mediterranean ingredients that I love – ratatouille from France, pesto from Italy and feta cheese from Greece. I am sure that you will agree that it is a winning combination! A tossed Greek salad and some crusty French or ciabatta bread would be ideal accompaniments.

30 ml (2 tbsp) olive oil
4 shallots, peeled and finely diced
3 cloves garlic, peeled and crushed
1 large red pepper, de-seeded and diced
2 courgettes, diced
2 aubergines, diced
225 g (8 oz) button mushrooms, sliced
425 g (15 oz) can chopped tomatoes

30 ml (2 tbsp) tomato purée
15 ml (1 tbsp) pesto
salt and fresh ground black pepper
55 g (2 oz) each butter and flour
570 ml (1 pint) cold milk
115 g (4 oz) feta cheese, crumbled
2 large eggs, separated

1. Pre-heat the oven to 180°C, 355°F, Gas 4. Fry shallots and garlic in the oil over a low heat for a few minutes to soften. Increase the heat and add pepper, courgettes, aubergines and mushrooms. Fry for a few minutes, stirring occasionally. Add tomatoes, tomato purée and pesto. Bring to the boil, season and simmer, covered, for 15 mins. Spoon into a large casserole dish.
2. Meanwhile, make the white sauce by whisking the butter, flour and milk together in a saucepan over a medium heat until it thickens and then simmer gently for 3–4 mins. Remove from the heat and stir in the feta cheese and egg yolks. Season with just pepper. Whisk the egg whites until stiff and fold gently into the cheese sauce. Spoon over the vegetables and bake in the oven for 50 mins until the top has risen like a soufflé and is golden brown. Serve at once.

ROASTED RATATOUILLE STUFFED MUSHROOMS

Serves 4

I saw giant stuffed mushrooms on display in a delicatessen in Chobham and they inspired me to create this dish. It is pure indulgence, as it is full of my favourite ingredients. Serve with SUN-DRIED TOMATO SAUCE *(page 70).*

4 very large mushrooms
1 small aubergine, cut into 2.5 cm (1 inch) dice
1 large courgette, cut into 2.5 cm (1 inch) dice
1 small red pepper, de-seeded and cut into 2.5 cm (1 inch) dice
1 small yellow pepper, de-seeded and cut into 2.5 cm (1 inch) dice
1 medium onion, peeled and roughly chopped
225 g (8 oz) cherry tomatoes
2 fat cloves garlic, finely chopped
30 ml (2 tbsp) olive oil
1 handful fresh basil leaves
55 g (2 oz) Gruyère cheese, grated

1. Pre-heat the oven to its highest setting. Sprinkle salt over the aubergines and courgettes, top up with a weight and leave for about an hour. Rinse and dry thoroughly in a clean cloth.
2. Arrange the aubergines, courgettes, peppers, onion and tomatoes in a large roasting tin and sprinkle the garlic over. Tear the basil leaves and sprinkle these over also. Drizzle the olive oil over and toss to make sure the vegetables are evenly coated. Season generously with salt and fresh black pepper.
3. Roast for 30–40 mins until the vegetables are cooked and tinged brown at the edges. Loosen the vegetables from the base of the tin.
4. Reduce the oven temperature to 200°C, 390°F, Gas 6.
5. Lightly oil the undersides of the mushrooms and the baking sheet or individual gratin dishes. Pile the 'ratatouille' into the cavities and then sprinkle the cheese on top. Cover loosely with foil and bake in the oven for 25–30 mins, removing the foil for the last few minutes so that the cheese can brown.

TUSCAN BAKE

Sainsbury once published a recipe which used fresh ravioli as a layer instead of lasagne. This gave me the idea for creating this dish. You could use mushroom or cheese ravioli instead of the spinach and Ricotta, and mushrooms could replace the peppers if using mushroom ravioli.

I recently served this recipe at a fund-raising supper for Mencap and it was a huge success. It freezes, either cooked or uncooked, very satisfactorily.

1 large aubergine, sliced fairly thin	395 g (14 oz) can chopped tomatoes
1 large courgette,	5 ml (1 tsp) pesto sauce
sliced thinly lengthways	15 ml (1 tbsp) tomato purée
2 red peppers, de-seeded and quartered	2.5 ml ($^1/_2$ tsp) sugar
60 ml (4 tbsp) olive oil	170 g (6 oz) Mozzarella cheese,
1 onion, finely chopped	sliced thinly
2 cloves garlic, peeled	225 g (8 oz) Ricotta cheese
and finely chopped	55 g (2 oz) Parmesan cheese,
10 ml (2 tsp) fresh thyme	freshly grated
or 2.5 ml ($^1/_2$ tsp) dried thyme)	250 g (9 oz) pack fresh spinach
15 ml (1 tbsp) finely chopped fresh parsley	and Ricotta ravioli

1. Sprinkle the aubergines and courgettes with salt, cover and weigh down and leave for half an hour. Rinse and dry in a clean tea towel.
2. Grill the peppers until blackened. Put into a plastic bag to cool, and for the skins to loosen. Skin and slice thinly.
3. Pre-heat the oven to 190°C, 375°F, Gas 5.
4. Fry the onion in half the oil with the garlic, thyme and parsley, without browning. Add the tomatoes, pesto, tomato purée and sugar and bring to the boil. Reduce the heat and simmer gently for about 10 mins. Season with salt and black pepper.
5. While the sauce is simmering, fry the aubergine and courgette slices in the remaining oil until golden brown and tender. Drain on kitchen paper.
6. To assemble the dish, put one third of the sauce in the bottom of a large gratin dish (about 20.5 x 30.5 cm, 8 x 12 ins). Add half the ravioli in a single layer, being careful not to overlap, half the aubergine slices, half the pepper slices, and all the courgette slices and Ricotta cheese. Repeat with the remaining vegetables and sauce, finishing with a layer of sauce.
7. Cover with the Mozzarella cheese slices and sprinkle with the grated Parmesan cheese.
8. Bake in the oven for about 25 mins until golden and bubbling.

SPICY MUSHROOM CASSEROLE

Serves 4

Mushrooms tend to feature a lot in vegetarian cooking because they add substance to dishes, both in flavour and texture. In this dish, the mushrooms more than achieve these aims. The spices give the sauce a bit of a kick – it's up to you to adjust the quantities to suit your own tastes. You might find that a perfect accompaniment would be boiled basmati rice, garnished with some chopped fresh coriander.

30 ml (2 tbsp) olive oil
1 large onion, peeled and diced
2 large cloves garlic, peeled and crushed
7.5 ml (1$\frac{1}{2}$ tsp) coriander seeds
1 small red chilli, de-seeded
   and finely diced
625 g (1 lb 6 oz) mixed mushrooms
   (e.g. button, flat, chestnut, and
   chanterelles)

2.5 ml ($\frac{1}{2}$ tsp) harissa
395 g (14 oz) can chopped tomatoes
5 ml (1 tsp) sugar
15 ml (1 tbsp) tomato purée
3 sun-dried tomatoes,
   finely chopped (optional)
15 ml (1 tbsp) fresh coriander, chopped
5 ml (1 tsp) balsamic vinegar
salt and fresh ground black pepper

1. Fry the onion and the garlic in the oil over a gentle heat for a few minutes to soften. Add the coriander seeds and chilli and stir to mix thoroughly. Stir in the mushrooms and coat all of them in the spiced onion. Then add the harissa, the tomatoes, sugar, tomato purée and the sun-dried tomatoes, if using.
2. Bring to the boil, lower the heat and simmer, covered, for 10 mins. Add the coriander leaves, balsamic vinegar and seasoning.

ROOT VEGETABLE RAGOUT

Serves 4–6

This is a hearty winter casserole which the family will love but is also suitable for entertaining. Jacket or mashed potatoes, both with lashings of butter, and a green vegetable are all that are needed to accompany it.

1 onion, finely chopped
1 clove garlic, peeled and crushed
45 g (1$\frac{1}{2}$ oz) butter
45 g (1$\frac{1}{2}$ oz) plain flour
2 large carrots, peeled
2 medium parsnips, peeled
2 medium sweet potatoes, peeled

1 large leek, trimmed and cut
   into thick slices
570 ml (1 pint) good vegetable stock
45 ml (3 tbsp) sherry
15 ml (1 tbsp) fresh parsley, finely
   chopped
100 g (3$\frac{1}{2}$ oz) fresh parsley

1. Cut the carrots, parsnips and the sweet potatoes into 2.5 cm (1 inch) cubes. Melt the butter in a large thick-bottomed saucepan and then fry the onion and garlic over a low heat to soften. Add the carrots, parsnips, sweet potatoes and leek and stir well so that all the vegetables are coated in the buttery onions. Cook over a low heat for a few minutes, stirring from time to time.
2. Stir in the flour thoroughly and cook for a few minutes. Add the stock, sherry, salt and black pepper and parsley and bring to the boil. Reduce the heat, place a lid on the saucepan and simmer gently for 30–40 mins until the vegetables are tender. Add the Boursin and stir until it has melted.
3. Check the seasoning before serving.

SPRING VEGETABLES AND TAGLIATELLE IN A PESTO SAUCE

Serves 4

When fresh asparagus appears in the shops, I feel that spring has arrived. This dish is perfect for serving at the start of spring when you no longer want to serve hearty winter meals – it is light and fresh yet full of flavour.

30 ml (2 tbsp) extra virgin olive oil
30 g (1 oz) butter
1 onion, peeled and finely chopped
100 g (3½ oz) packet asparagus tips
200 g (7 oz) packet baby corn (cut in half lengthways) and mangetout
115 g (4 oz) mushrooms, button or oyster, sliced

200 ml (7 fl oz) crème fraiche
30 ml (2 tbsp) pesto sauce
450 g (1 lb) tagliatelle, ideally a mixture of plain and green
fresh shavings of Parmesan cheese
15 ml (1 tbsp) pine nuts, lightly toasted
salt and fresh ground black pepper

1. Heat the oil and butter together in a large frying pan and gently fry the onion until it is cooked but not coloured. While the onion is cooking, blanch the asparagus and baby corn in boiling water for 2 mins and then drain thoroughly.
2. Add the mushrooms to the onion and continue to cook for a couple of minutes until they begin to soften. Add the asparagus, baby corn and mangetouts and cook until just tender. Stir in the crème fraiche and pesto sauce and season with salt and pepper.
3. While the vegetables are cooking, cook the tagliatelle according to the pack instructions. Drain thoroughly and then tip onto a large serving platter or individual plates and spoon the vegetable sauce on top. Sprinkle with the Parmesan and pine nuts, if using.

VEGETABLE BALTI

Serves 4–6

You can vary the ingredients of this curry to suit your tastes. I think that the root vegetables work well as they retain their shape and add substance. I serve it with some basmati rice and garlic and coriander naan bread to mop up the delicious 'gravy'.

1 onion, peeled and chopped
2 garlic cloves, peeled and chopped
2.5 cm (1 inch) piece fresh root ginger, peeled and grated
3 cardamom pods, crushed
30 ml (2 tbsp) sunflower oil
15 ml (1 tbsp) Balti curry paste
15 ml (1 tbsp) tomato purée
395 g (14 oz) can chopped tomatoes
115 g (4 oz) red lentils

225 g (8 oz) sweet potatoes, peeled and cubed
225 g (8 oz) small button mushrooms
425 g (15 oz) can chick peas, drained
5 ml (1 tsp) each ground coriander, cinnamon, cumin and turmeric
salt and pepper
570 ml (1 pint) vegetable stock
30 ml (2 tbsp) freshly chopped coriander

1. Fry the onion, garlic, ginger and cardamom pods in the oil for 5 mins. Add the Balti paste, mix in thoroughly. Add the remaining ingredients except for the fresh coriander. Bring to the boil. Cover and simmer for 20 mins, stirring occasionally.
2. Stir in the fresh coriander and cook, uncovered, for a further 10 mins by which time the sauce should have thickened considerably.

Non-vegetarian tip: Any diced meat could be added before the Balti paste is stirred in but the cooking time will need to be extended until the meat is tender.

CELERIAC AND SWEET POTATO 'TOAD IN THE HOLE'

Serves 6

This is real comfort food and it can be served to both meat eaters and vegetarians simply by including the appropriate sausages. You could serve it with gravy, but I prefer to serve it with MUSHROOM AND WHITE WINE SAUCE (page 67).

12 vegetarian sausages
450 g (1 lb) celeriac, peeled and cubed
795 g (1 lb 12 oz) sweet potatoes, peeled and cubed

55 g (2 oz) Stilton cheese, cubed
225 g (8 oz) puff pastry
1 egg, lightly beaten
salt and fresh ground black pepper

1. Pre-heat the oven to 220°C, 430°F, Gas 7.
2. Place the celeriac and potatoes in a saucepan, cover with water, bring to the boil, cover and simmer for 20 mins until both vegetables are tender.

3. Meanwhile, roll out the pastry and cut out into 12.5 cm (5 ins) circles, place on a baking sheet, brush with the egg and bake in the oven for about 20 mins until risen and golden brown. Fry or grill the sausages until golden brown.
4. Drain the vegetables, mash until there are no lumps, stir in the Stilton cheese until it has melted and season well.
5. To serve, place a big 'dollop' of mash in the centre of each plate (warm), flatten a little with the back of the spoon, place two sausages side by side in the centre, place the pastry lid on top. Surround with the mushroom and white wine sauce.

Non-vegetarian tip: Use any meat sausages of your choice.

VEGETABLE FILO PARCELS   Serves 6

These parcels look very impressive. You could make one large parcel and present it on an oval platter. Whichever way you choose, serve it with a rich tomato sauce, preferably made with ripe fresh tomatoes.

30 ml (2 tbsp) olive oil (ideally from the jar of sun-dried tomatoes)
1 large onion, chopped
2 cloves garlic, peeled and chopped
225 g (8 oz) aubergine, cut into small dice
1 large courgette, cut into small dice
2 sticks celery, cut into small slices
115 g (4 oz) button mushrooms, sliced
1 large red pepper, de-seeded and cut into small dice

115 ml (4 fl oz) red wine
4 sun-dried tomatoes, finely chopped
10 ml (2 tsp) pesto
10 ml (2 tsp) paprika
6 fresh basil leaves, shredded
15 ml (1 tbsp) pine nuts, lightly toasted
60 ml (4 tbsp) single cream
salt and fresh ground black pepper
85 g (3 oz) feta cheese, crumbled
12 sheets filo pastry (about 285 g, 10 oz)
55 g (2 oz) butter, melted

1. Pre-heat the oven to 190°C, 375°F, Gas 5.
2. Fry the onion and garlic gently in the oil for about 2 mins. Add aubergine, courgette, celery, mushrooms and pepper and continue to sauté for about 5 mins to soften slightly. Add red wine, tomatoes, pesto, paprika and basil. Continue to cook until all the liquid has evaporated. Season with salt and pepper and fold in the pine nuts and cream. Allow to cool. Fold in the feta cheese.
3. Lay 6 sheets filo pastry on the work surface and brush with melted butter. Lay remaining sheets on top and brush with butter. Spoon vegetable mixture along one narrow end of each rectangle, leaving a 4 cm (1½ ins) gap at either side. Fold into a parcel and place on a baking sheet. Brush with remaining butter. Bake for approximately 20 mins until the pastry is crisp and golden brown.

DRAGEMIROFF FRICASSEE

Serves 4

This is a Russian dish which is traditionally made using cooked left-over chicken. Here, the chicken is replaced by Quorn – if you are not a fan of meat substitutes, you could simply use extra mushrooms. Serve with basmati rice and a tossed green salad.

30 g (1 oz) butter
1 onion, finely chopped
1 clove garlic, peeled and chopped
115 g (4 oz) button mushrooms, sliced
340 g (12 oz) Quorn pieces
10 ml (2 tsp) fresh tarragon
    or 5 ml (1 tsp) freeze-dried

10 ml (2 tsp) sugar
75 ml (5 tbsp) good vegetable stock
30 ml (2 tbsp) Amontillado sherry
7.5 ml (1$^{1}/_{2}$ tsp) cornflour
140 ml ($^{1}/_{4}$ pint) soured cream
    or Greek yoghurt
salt and fresh ground black pepper

1. Melt the butter in a saucepan and fry the onion and garlic over a gentle heat until softened. Add the mushrooms and Quorn and continue to cook for a few more minutes. Add the tarragon, sugar, stock and the sherry. Season well and bring to the boil. Simmer for a couple of minutes.
2. Dilute the cornflour with a little cold water. Add to the pan followed by the soured cream or Greek yoghurt. Return to a gentle simmer and check the seasoning. Serve with rice.

Non-vegetarian tip: Replace the Quorn with cooked diced chicken.

MOUSSAKA

Serves 4–6

This version of moussaka was prepared for me at a hotel near Wells, Somerset. It was so delicious that I asked for the recipe. Using feta cheese in the topping gives it an authentic Greek flavour.

2 aubergine sliced into
    medium thick rounds
30 ml (2 tbsp) olive oil plus extra
1 large onion, peeled and chopped
2 cloves garlic, peeled and chopped
285 g (10 oz) button mushrooms, sliced
395 g (14 oz) can chopped tomatoes
30 ml (2 tbsp) tomato purée
200 ml (7 fl oz) red wine

15 ml (1 tbsp) chopped fresh thyme
7.5 ml (1$^{1}/_{2}$ tsp) cinnamon
salt and fresh ground black pepper
30 g (1 oz) butter
30 g (1 oz) flour
285 ml ($^{1}/_{2}$ pint) milk
2 eggs, beaten
a little freshly grated nutmeg
100 g (3$^{1}/_{2}$ oz) feta cheese, crumbled

1. Pre-heat the grill. Lightly brush the aubergine slices with some oil and grill until golden brown and softened.
2. Fry the onion and garlic in the 30 ml (2 tbsp) olive oil until softened. Add the mushrooms and cook for a few minutes more. Add the tomatoes, tomato purée, red wine, thyme and cinnamon. Season with salt and pepper. Bring to the boil and then simmer gently for 10–15 mins.
3. While the tomato sauce is cooking, make the cheese sauce. Place the butter, flour and milk in a saucepan. Bring to the boil while stirring continuously. Simmer very gently for a couple of minutes.
4. Remove from the heat and whisk in the eggs, followed by the cheese. Season with pepper.
5. Pre-heat the oven to 180°C, 355°F, Gas 4.
6. To assemble, place a third of the tomato sauce in the base of a large gratin dish. Add half the aubergines, followed by a third of the sauce, the remaining aubergine, the rest of the sauce and top with the cheese sauce.
7. Bake in the oven for 25–30 mins until the top is golden brown and the sauce bubbling around the edges.

MUSHROOMS IN RED WINE SAUCE WITH TAGLIATELLE
Serves 4

This sauce has a very intense flavour so you simply need a tossed green salad to accompany it.

55 g (2 oz) butter
450 g (1 lb) chestnut mushrooms,
   wiped and sliced thickly
3 plum tomatoes, skinned,
   de-seeded and chopped
140 ml ($^1/_4$ pint) good vegetable stock

140 ml ($^1/_4$ pint) red wine
salt and fresh ground black pepper
680 g (1$^1/_2$ lb) dried tagliatelle
Parmesan shavings
crème fraiche

1. Melt the butter in a saucepan and fry the mushrooms for a couple of minutes. Add the chopped tomatoes and cook for another couple of minutes. Add the stock and wine. Season with salt and pepper and bring to the boil. Simmer for about 5 mins. Pour half the sauce into a food processor or blender and purée until quite smooth. Stir in the remaining sauce and reheat. Check the seasoning.
2. While the sauce is cooking, cook the tagliatelle in plenty of boiling salted water for the length of time stated on the packet. Drain well and transfer to a warm serving bowl or plates. Pour over the sauce. Place spoonfuls of crème fraiche on top and sprinkle with the Parmesan shavings.

GOURMET LASAGNE

Vegetarian lasagne has a poor reputation: so often it is a tasteless sludgy mess. If it is cooked well, and if you use quality ingredients, lasagne becomes a superb dish. Don't be put off by the lengthy ingredient list and method of preparation – once the lasagne is prepared, it can be left in the fridge until you are ready to bake it, which is a great advantage when you are entertaining.

225 g (8 oz) aubergine, cut into fairly thick slices
450 g (1 lb) courgettes, cut into fairly thick slices
2 red peppers, de-seeded and cut into 2.5 cm (1 inch) cubes
2 large onions, peeled – one of them cut into chunks
    and the other finely diced
6 sun-dried tomatoes, cut into thin strips
60 ml (4 tbsp) olive oil, from the sun-dried tomatoes, ideally
2 large cloves garlic, crushed
395 g (14 oz) can tomatoes
15 ml (1 tbsp) tomato purée
30 ml (2 tbsp) pine nuts, toasted
30 g (1 oz) each of butter and plain flour
285 ml ($^{1}/_{2}$ pint) milk
10 ml (2 tsp / 1 dessertspn) pesto
6 sheets lasagne
55 g (2 oz) freshly grated Parmesan cheese
130 g ($4^{1}/_{2}$ oz) Mozzarella cheese, thinly sliced
salt and fresh ground black pepper

1. Pre-heat the oven to its hottest setting. Place the aubergine, courgettes, peppers, onion chunks and sun-dried tomatoes in a large roasting tin, drizzle over half the oil and sprinkle over half the garlic. Toss well (I use my hands!) and bake in the oven for about half an hour until the edges of the vegetables are looking charred. It is worth stirring them half way through the cooking.
2. Put to one side. Reduce the oven to 180°C, 355°F, Gas 4.
3. Make the tomato sauce by frying the diced onion and remaining garlic in the rest of the oil for a few minutes.
4. Add the can of tomatoes, tomato purée and seasoning. Bring to the boil and simmer for 10–15 mins.
5. While the sauce is simmering, make the pesto sauce by whisking the butter, flour and milk together continuously until it has thickened and come to the boil. Season well and simmer very gently for 5 mins. Remove from the heat and stir in the pesto sauce.

6. To assemble, spoon half the tomato sauce evenly over the base of a large gratin dish, arrange half the lasagne sheets on top, followed by half the roasted vegetables. Continue the layering with the rest of the tomato sauce, all the Mozzarella, the rest of the vegetables, the pine nuts, the rest of the lasagne and then spread all the pesto sauce over the lasagne sheets making sure they are completely covered.
7. Sprinkle the Parmesan cheese all over the sauce and bake in the oven for about half an hour until the sauce is bubbling and the top golden brown.

CELERIAC AND LEEK PLAIT   Serves 6–8

This plait makes an impressive dish but is very straightforward to make. A roasted red pepper sauce is an ideal accompaniment as it provides colour and contrasting flavour but any favourite sauce or gravy could be served.

30 g (1 oz) butter
1 celeriac weighing about 450 g (1 lb), peeled and cubed
30 ml (2 tbsp) dry white wine
2 small leeks, trimmed and cut into thick slices
1 red pepper, halved and de-seeded

115 g (4 oz) Stilton cheese, diced
2 large eggs, lightly beaten
100 ml (3¹/₂ fl oz) crème fraiche
395 g (14 oz) puff pastry
1 egg, beaten, to glaze
salt and fresh ground black pepper
15 ml (1 tbsp) sesame seeds (optional)

1. Melt the butter in a saucepan and gently cook the celeriac until fairly soft. Add the wine and continue to cook for a further 10 mins until tender, stirring from time to time. Leave to cool a little and then purée with the eggs and crème fraiche, seasoning well.
2. Cook the leeks in a little water until tender, drain and reserve.
3. Meanwhile grill the peppers until charred, place in a plastic bag, leave to cool.
4. Add the leeks and Stilton to the celeriac purée. When the pepper has cooled, peel it and cut into thin strips and fold them into the celeriac purée also.
5. Pre-heat the oven to 200°C, 390°F, Gas 6.
6. On a lightly floured surface, roll out the pastry to a 28 x 18cm (11 x 7 ins) rectangle and place on a lightly greased baking sheet of at least 30.5 x 20.5 cm (12 x 8 ins) size. Place the celeriac filling down the centre.
7. Cut the pastry on either side of the filling into 2.5 cm (1 inch) strips, leaving at least 1.25 cm (¹/₂ inch) uncut on either side. Brush the strips with a little of the beaten egg and then use the strips to overlap the filling to form a plait.
8. Brush with the rest of the egg and sprinkle with sesame seeds, if using. Bake in the oven for about 20 mins until golden brown.

SINGAPORE NOODLES

Serves 4–6

This dish can be cooked in minutes, ideal for an informal dinner without spending hours in the kitchen. Vary the vegetables to suit your tastes and availability. Remember to cook those needing more cooking before adding the remaining ingredients.

$^1/_2$ packet medium egg noodles
60 ml (4 tbsp) sunflower oil
2 cloves garlic, peeled and crushed
170 g (6 oz) oyster or button mushrooms
$^1/_2$ bunch spring onions,
   trimmed and finely chopped
115 g (4 oz) beansprouts
10 ml (2 tsp) lemon juice

45 ml (3 tbsp) Thai stir-fry sauce
115 g (4 oz) baby corn, sliced lengthways
115 g (4 oz) sugar snap peas
15 ml (1 tbsp) caster sugar
45 g ($1^1/_2$ oz) cashew nuts
30 g (1 oz) packet coriander
salt and fresh ground black pepper

1. Cover the noodles with boiling water and leave to stand for 5 mins. Rinse thoroughly in cold water and leave to drain.
2. Heat the oil in a wok or large frying pan and stir-fry the garlic, mushrooms, onions, corn and sugar snap peas over a high heat for about 4 mins stirring all the time. Add the beansprouts, lemon juice and Thai sauce.
3. Add the noodles and toss all the ingredients together using two forks. Add the sugar, cashew nuts and coriander and season well, to taste. Serve straight away on warm plates.

Non-vegetarian tip: Thin strips of beef or chicken could be included and cooked with the vegetables.

BEAN AND PESTO CASSEROLE

Serves 4

This is a hearty casserole full of flavour. It takes very little time to prepare by using tinned beans. All you need to accompany it are jacket potatoes and a green vegetable such as French beans or broccoli.

30 ml (2 tbsp) olive oil
1 large onion, peeled
   and finely chopped
2 cloves garlic, peeled and chopped
2 carrots, peeled and sliced
130 g ($4^1/_2$ oz) mushrooms, cut in chunks
395 g (14 oz) can chopped tomatoes

15 ml (1 tbsp) tomato purée
285 ml ($^1/_2$ pint) red wine
salt and fresh ground black pepper
300 g ($10^1/_2$ oz) can each of borlotti
   and cannelini beans
395 g (14 oz) can black-eyed beans
45 ml (3 tbsp) pesto sauce

1. Fry the onion and garlic in the oil over a gentle heat for a few minutes until the onion has softened. Add the carrots and mushrooms and cook for a few more minutes. Add the chopped tomatoes, tomato purée, three types of beans, red wine and season well.
2. Bring to the boil, cover and simmer for 20–25 mins until the carrots are tender. Stir in the pesto sauce and simmer for a few more minutes. Check the seasoning and serve.

PEA AND MUSHROOM RISOTTO   Serves 4

Risottos are real comfort food. It is important to use the right rice otherwise it simply won't work. You can vary the flavourings, e.g. asparagus, spinach, artichoke, tomatoes. Use a really good stock – a home-made one will give the best flavour to the risotto.

15 g ($^1/_2$ oz) dried porcini mushrooms
570 ml (1 pint) hot water
55 g (2 oz) butter
1 large onion, peeled and finely diced
340 g (12 oz) Arborio risotto rice
250 g (9 oz) chestnut or portabello
   mushrooms, wiped and cut
   into chunks

140 ml ($^1/_4$ pint) dry white wine
1 litre (1$^3/_4$ pints) hot vegetable stock
115 g (4 oz) frozen garden peas
45 ml (3 tbsp) finely chopped fresh parsley
55 g (2 oz) freshly grated Parmesan
   cheese, plus extra to serve
salt and fresh ground black pepper

1. First of all, soak the dried mushrooms in the hot water for half and hour.
2. Meanwhile, melt the butter in a large saucepan and fry the onion for a few minutes until soft and golden brown. Add the rice and cook for about 5 mins, stirring frequently, until the grains are translucent. Add the mushrooms and stir to coat them in the oil. Cook for a few more minutes until they have begun to soften.
3. Turn up the heat and add the wine. Boil rapidly for a few minutes.
4. Drain the dried mushrooms, reserving the liquid, chop them and add them to the risotto. Add some of the reserved mushroom liquid to the risotto and stir until it has been absorbed. Continue to add the liquid, followed by the stock, stirring often, until it has all been absorbed and the consistency is a bit soupy. The grains should be tender but still have a little bite. Add the peas and cook for a couple of minutes.
5. Season with salt and pepper.
6. Remove the saucepan from the heat and stir in the parsley and Parmesan cheese. Then spoon onto *warm* serving plates and sprinkle with the extra Parmesan cheese.

LEEK, MUSHROOM AND TOFU CRUMBLE   Serves 4–6

Leeks and mushrooms are perfect partners. In this dish, they are combined in a creamy wine sauce and topped with a savoury crumble. I like to serve it with jacket potatoes and a green vegetable such as broccoli.

565 g (1¼ lb) leeks, trimmed and cut into thick slices
450 g (1 lb) button mushrooms,
   cut in quarters or halves, depending on size
55 g (2 oz) butter
15 g (½ oz) dried porcini mushrooms,
   soaked in 140 ml (¼ pint) hot water for ½ hour
140 ml (¼ pint) dry white wine
140 ml (¼ pint) milk
285 g (10 oz) packet original tofu, cut into 2.5 cm (1 inch) cubes
55 g (2 oz) plain flour
85 g (3 oz) grated Cheddar cheese
55 g (2 oz) wholemeal breadcrumbs
15 ml (1 tbsp) fresh parsley, finely chopped
15 g (½ oz) pine kernels
salt and fresh ground black pepper

1. Melt half the butter in one saucepan and the remainder in another. Fry leeks gently in one and button mushrooms in the other until they are soft.
2. Strain the dried mushrooms, reserving the liquid. Add them to the button mushrooms, stir in the flour and cook gently for a couple of minutes. Gradually add the reserved liquid, the wine and milk. Bring to the boil, stirring all the time. Simmer for a couple of minutes and then stir in the leeks, half the cheese and tofu. Season to taste. Pre-heat the oven to180°C, 355°F, Gas 4.
3. Spoon the mixture into a large gratin dish. Combine the breadcrumbs, the remaining cheese, parsley and pine kernels. Season and sprinkle over the vegetables and tofu. Bake in the oven for about 25 mins until the topping is crisp and golden brown

WINTER VEGETABLE AND STILTON CRUMBLE

Serves 6

My friend, Tanya, cooked this dish for me at a dinner party, having tasted a similar dish at a pub. I loved it so much that I asked if I could include it in this book.
A jacket potato and some green vegetables are all that is needed to accompany it.

15 ml (1 tbsp) olive oil
1 medium onion, peeled and diced
2 cloves garlic, peeled and crushed
3 medium leeks, trimmed and cut into thick slices
3 medium parsnips, peeled and cut into 2.5 cm (1 inch) cubes
1 small celeriac, peeled and cut into 2.5 cm (1 inch) cubes
285 g (10 oz) chestnut mushrooms, halved if large
140 ml ($^1/_4$ pint) good vegetable stock
285 ml ($^1/_2$ pint) dry white wine
22.5 ml ($1^1/_2$ tbsp) cornflour dissolved in a little water
140 ml ($^1/_4$ pint) single cream
115 g (4 oz) cream cheese
85 g (3 oz) Stilton cheese, cubed
70 g ($2^1/_2$ oz) Parmesan cheese, freshly grated
70 g ($2^1/_2$ oz) fresh wholemeal breadcrumbs

1. Fry the onion and garlic in the oil until soft but not coloured. Add the leeks, parsnips and celeriac and cook gently for a few minutes. Add the mushrooms and cook for a few more minutes. Add the stock and dry white wine, bring to the boil and then simmer gently for about 15 mins until the vegetables have softened but still retain their shape.
2. Meanwhile, pre-heat the oven to 190ºC , 375ºF, Gas 5. Stir in the dissolved cornflour to the vegetable mixture and stir until thickened. Add the cream, cream cheese and Stilton and stir until dissolved.
3. Spoon into a large oven-proof dish, sprinkle on the Parmesan cheese and breadcrumbs which have been mixed together and bake in the oven for 30–40 mins until the sauce is bubbling and the top golden brown.

DESSERTS

APPLE AND SULTANA SURPRISE PUDDING   Serves 4–6

This is a variation on lemon surprise pudding where a sauce gathers underneath during cooking. Here, the lemon sauce mixes in with some Bramley apples and sultanas – a lovely combination!

680 g (1¹/₂ lb) Bramley apples, peeled, cored and sliced	**30 g (1 oz) butter, softened**
30 ml (2 tbsp) granulated sugar	**115 g (4 oz) soft brown sugar**
60 ml (4 tbsp) water	**1 lemon, rind and juice**
squeeze lemon juice	**30 g (1 oz) plain flour**
	2 large eggs, separated

1. Place the first four ingredients in a saucepan and bring to the boil and then simmer very gently until the apples are soft but retain their shape. Spoon them into a greased 1.1 litre (2 pint) soufflé dish.
2. Pre-heat the oven to 180°C, 355°F, Gas 4.
3. Cream the butter with half the sugar, then beat in the yolks, rind, remaining sugar and flour and finally the lemon juice. Whisk the egg whites until stiff, fold in one tablespoon into the mixture to loosen it and then gently fold in the remaining whites.
4. Spoon the sponge mixture over the apples and bake in the oven in a roasting tin, half filled with hot water, for 35–40 mins until the sponge is firm to the touch and golden brown. Serve with cream or really good vanilla ice cream.

CHOCOLATE MOUSSE WITH ORANGE SYLLABUB

Serves 6

Chocolate and oranges go extremely well together. Slices of fresh oranges under the chocolate mousse are a perfect contrast to the richness of the mousse and syllabub.

115 g (4 oz) plain chocolate
285 ml (½ pint) double cream
3 oranges

45 g (1½ oz) caster sugar
15 ml (1 tbsp) Cointreau
grated chocolate

1. Break the chocolate into pieces and place in a bowl with 30 ml (2 tbsp) water over a bowl of simmering water and allow to melt, stirring occasionally. Allow to cool. Add the grated rind from 2 oranges and fold in half the cream, which has been lightly whipped.
2. Peel both oranges and slice between the membrane. Divide between 6 glasses.
3. Spoon the chocolate mousse on top and refrigerate until set.
4. Combine the juice from the third orange with the sugar and Cointreau in a large bowl and leave for half an hour for the flavours to develop. Stir in the remaining cream and whisk until the mixture just holds its shape (it will continue to thicken in the fridge).
5. Spoon onto the chocolate mousse and sprinkle over a little grated chocolate.

MANGO SYLLABUB

Serves 4–6

Mangoes are ideal to eat after spicy food. I created this recipe to follow an Indian meal. Vary the fruit in this syllabub to suit your tastes – you could substitute apricots or peaches very successfully. I like to serve it with crisp dessert biscuits.

1 lemon, grated rind and juice
30 ml (2 tbsp) sherry
30 ml (2 tbsp) brandy
30 ml (2 tbsp) icing sugar

2 large ripe mangoes, peeled and stoned
or 2 cans mango slices, drained
225 ml (8 fl oz) double cream

1. Mix the lemon rind and juice into the sherry, brandy and sugar, then set aside for a short while.
2. Put the mango flesh into a food processor, then blend to make a purée. Divide the purée between tall serving glasses and place in the fridge to chill.
3. Place the cream in a bowl and strain the brandy mixture over it, discarding the rind. Whisk it until soft peaks form (be careful not to over-whisk as the mixture will continue to thicken in the fridge). Spoon or pipe over the mango purée. Cover with cling film and return to the fridge until ready to serve.

APRICOT AND CHOCOLATE CHIFLE

Serves 8

I have called this dessert a chifle because it is a cross between a cheesecake and a trifle and I have to say it is a winning combination!

4 trifle sponges
45 ml (3 tbsp) brandy
410 g (14¹/₂ oz) can apricot halves,
    in natural juice, drained
425 ml (³/₄ pint) custard
285 ml (¹/₂ pint) whipping cream, whipped

250 g (9 oz) cream cheese
55 g (2 oz) caster sugar
115 g (4 oz) plain chocolate,
    melted and cooled
cocoa powder for dusting

1. Cut the sponges into small pieces and place in the bottom of a glass/trifle serving bowl. Sprinkle the brandy over. Reserve two of the apricot halves and cut the remainder into small pieces. Spoon these over the sponge pieces.
2. Divide the custard between two large bowls. Add the cream cheese and half the sugar to one and mix thoroughly. Add the chocolate and remaining sugar to the other and mix well. Add half the cream to the chocolate mixture and fold in thoroughly.
3. Spoon the cream cheese mixture onto the apricots, levelling the surface and then repeat with the chocolate mixture. Spread the remaining cream on top, dust lightly with the cocoa powder and decorate with the remaining apricot halves which have been cut into thin slices.

BAKED RASPBERRY PUDDING

Serves 4–6

This simple yet delicious pudding can also be made with other berries such as blackberries and loganberries.

450 g (1 lb) raspberries
30 ml (2 tbsp) caster sugar
30 ml (2 tbsp) Kirsch (optional)

225 g (8 oz) thick Greek yoghurt
2 large eggs
15 ml (1 tbsp) plain flour

1. Pre-heat the oven to 150°C, 300°F, Gas 2.
2. Place raspberries in a shallow oven-proof dish, lightly greased. Sprinkle over half the sugar and place in the oven for a few minutes to warm through.
3. Beat yoghurt, eggs, flour and remaining sugar together. Remove raspberries from the oven, and sprinkle with the Kirsch, if using. Pour over the yoghurt mixture and bake in the oven for about 45 mins until firm and set.
4. Serve either hot or cold with cream or ice cream.

TOFFEE APPLE CHEESECAKE   Serves 8

I love serving this cheesecake at Halloween – the two key ingredients represent this time of year. It freezes very well and could be made in the September apple glut.

Base:
55 g (2 oz) butter, melted
115g (4 oz) digestive biscuits, crushed
30 g (1 oz) chopped hazelnuts, toasted

Filling:
225 g (8 oz) cream cheese
2 large eggs, separated
115 g (4 oz) caster sugar
$^1/_2$ lemon, grated rind and juice
140 ml ($^1/_4$ pint) soured cream

285 ml ($^1/_2$ pint) apple purée
pinch mixed spice
20 g ($^3/_4$ oz) gelatine
    or a vegetarian equivalent
120 ml (8 tbsp) apple juice

Topping:
85g (3 oz) toffee
85 ml (3 fl oz) milk
140 ml ($^1/_4$ pint) double cream

1 red skinned apple, cored and
    sliced thinly and dipped in diluted
    lemon juice

1. Combine the base ingredients and press into the base of a greased, loose-bottomed cake tin. Chill while making the filling.
2. Soften the cheese in a large bowl and then mix in the yolks, sugar, rind and juice, soured cream, apple purée and mixed spice.
3. Pour the apple juice into a bowl and sprinkle on the gelatine (follow the pack instructions for the vegetarian equivalent). Dissolve by stirring over a pan of hot water or by heating in a microwave on full power for 40–60 seconds (time depends on the power of your microwave). Leave to cool to a similar temperature as the cheese mixture. Beat thoroughly into the cheese mixture.
4. Whisk the whites until stiff. Fold one tablespoon into the cheese mixture to loosen it then gently fold in the remaining whites. Spoon onto the biscuit base and level the surface. Chill for at least three hours until firm and set.
5. To make the topping, put toffees and milk in a saucepan and melt gently, stirring frequently until the toffee melts.
6. Allow to cool thoroughly and fold in the cream which has been whipped.
7. Run a palette knife around the sides of the cheesecake to ease it away from the tin and then unclip the tin. If you are feeling brave, slide the knife under the base and slide the cheesecake onto a serving plate.
8. Spread toffee cream on top of the cheesecake. Decorate with the apple slices.

AMARETTI MOCHA CREAMS

Serves 4–6

This simple, light dessert would be an ideal end to a rich Italian meal. It can be made several hours in advance, so you can concentrate on the other course(s).

115 g (4 oz) Amaretti biscuits, roughly crushed
30 ml (2 tbsp) strong black coffee, preferably espresso
30 ml (2 tbsp) Tia Maria or Kahlua

285 ml (¹/₂ pint) whipping cream
285 ml (¹/₂ pint) Greek yoghurt
30 g (1 oz) demerara sugar
grated chocolate or chocolate-covered coffee beans (optional)

1. Combine the coffee and alcohol in a large bowl. Add the cream and whip until it just holds its shape and then fold in the Greek yoghurt and sugar.
2. Divide half the biscuits between stemmed glasses. Spoon half the mocha cream over the biscuits. Sprinkle the remaining biscuits on top followed by the rest of the cream mixture.
3. Chill until ready to serve.
4. Decorate with either Amaretti biscuits (whole or finely crushed), grated chocolate or chocolate-covered coffee beans.

WHISKY AND GINGER ICE CREAM

Serves 6

I once made too much whisky and ginger syllabub. Rather than throwing it away, I froze it and discovered that I had made a delicious ice cream! A BITTER CHOCOLATE SAUCE (page 71) is a perfect accompaniment.

30 ml (2 tbsp) whisky
30 ml (2 tbsp) ginger conserve
15 ml (1 tbsp) caster sugar
grated rind of 1 lemon

285 ml (¹/₂ pint) double cream, chilled
15 ml (1 tbsp) finely chopped, preserved ginger (optional, for stronger flavour)
2 egg whites, whisked stiffly

1. Combine the whisky, ginger conserve, sugar and lemon rind in a bowl and leave to infuse for at least 15 mins. Stir in the cream and whisk until thick. Add the preserved ginger, if using.
2. Fold in a small amount of the egg whites to loosen the mixture, then gently fold in the remaining egg whites.
3. Lightly oil a small (450 g, 1 lb) loaf tin and line with cling film. Spoon the mixture into the tin and freeze until solid.
4. Invert onto a plate and slice. Place onto plates and serve with the bitter chocolate sauce, preferably warmed.

MOCHA ALMOND GATEAU

Serves 6–8

The beauty of this gâteau is that it is not baked and can be prepared hours in advance. It freezes extremely well – I try and keep one in the freezer as it is a wonderful 'standby' pudding.

85 g (3 oz) unsalted butter
85 g (3 oz) caster sugar
115 g (4 oz) ground almonds
1 large egg yolk
85 ml (3 fl oz) single cream
55 g (2 oz) dried apricots,
    finely chopped

15 ml (1 tbsp) chocolate-covered coffee
    beans plus extra for decoration
45 ml (3 tbsp) brandy
140 ml ($\frac{1}{4}$ pint) strong black coffee
approx 24 sponge fingers
285 ml ($\frac{1}{2}$ pint) whipping cream, whipped
grated chocolate

1. Grease and line the base and narrow sides of a 450 g (1 lb) loaf tin.
2. Cream the butter and sugar together until light and fluffy. Add the yolk, almonds and single cream and beat until smooth. Fold in the apricots and coffee beans.
3. Combine the coffee and brandy. Dip a third of the sponge fingers, one at a time, into the coffee mixture and arrange in a row in the base of the tin. Spread half the almond mixture on top. Repeat the layers once more, then finish with the sponge fingers. Chill in the fridge to set.
4. Turn out onto a serving dish. Spread two-thirds of the cream all over the gâteau. Pipe the remaining cream on top and decorate with a sprinkling of grated chocolate and some chocolate-coated coffee beans.

DATE AND WALNUT RICE PUDDING BRULEE

Serves 4

This dessert is made from store cupboard ingredients and takes minutes to make. Guests will think that you have spent ages preparing it! You can vary the flavourings to suit your tastes and what you have in your cupboard.

425 g (15 oz) can creamed rice pudding
30 ml (2 tbsp) crème fraiche
4 stoned dried dates, chopped

4 walnut halves, chopped
60 ml (4 tbsp) demerara sugar

1. Combine the rice pudding, crème fraiche, dates and walnuts in a bowl and then spoon into four ramekin dishes.
2. Pre-heat the grill. Sprinkle the demerara sugar evenly over the surface of the rice mixture and grill until the sugar has caramelised. Chill until ready to serve.

CHOCOLATE TRUFFLE TERRINE

Serves 6–8

I adore Belgian chocolate truffles. This pudding is meant to resemble the gooey centre of really decadent truffles. It is very rich and should be served in fairly thin slices, with a RASPBERRY COULIS (page 71).

115 g (4 oz) good quality plain
   chocolate, broken into pieces
225 g (8 oz) mascarpone cheese
7.5 ml (½ tbsp) coffee granules
15 ml (1 tbsp) coffee liqueur, e.g. Kahlua

15 ml (1 tbsp) cocoa, sieved
140 ml (¼ pint) whipping cream
8 sponge fingers
140 ml (¼ pint) approx. strong black
   coffee, cooled

1. Lightly oil a small (450 g, 1 lb) loaf tin and line with cling film.
2. Place the chocolate, the coffee granules and 15 ml (1 tbsp) hot water in a bowl and place the bowl over a pan of hot water, making sure that there are no gaps for steam to escape and cause the chocolate to seize. Leave until the chocolate has melted (stirring from time to time), then cool slightly.
3. Fold the melted chocolate into the mascarpone cheese with the liqueur and cocoa powder. Gently fold in the cream.
4. Spoon half the mixture into the tin, and level the surface. Dip the sponge fingers into the coffee so that they are soaked, being careful not to let them disintegrate, and arrange them side by side on top of the chocolate mixture. Spoon on the remaining mixture, level the surface again, and chill in the fridge to set.
5. To serve, un-mould the terrine, cut into slices, place on plates and surround with raspberry coulis.

CREAMY APRICOT BOMBE

Serves 8

This is a very versatile pudding: in the winter, I decorate it with clementines and physallis and in the summer with a mixture of summer berries.

225 g (8 oz) cream cheese
85 g (3 oz) caster sugar
85 g (3 oz) unsalted butter, melted
170 g (6 oz) dried apricots,
   cut into small pieces
55 g (2 oz) chopped hazelnuts, toasted
2 oranges, grated rind and juice

1 lemon, grated rind and juice
8 trifle sponges, each cut
   horizontally into three
1 sachet gelatine or 15 ml (3 tsp)
   vegetarian equivalent
140 ml (¼ pint) whipping cream, whipped
selection of seasonal fruit

1. Combine the cream cheese, sugar and butter and mix well. Fold in the apricots, nuts and citrus rinds.
2. Dissolve the gelatine or vegetarian equivalent in 30 ml (2 tbsp) water over a pan of hot water or by heating in the microwave for 20 seconds. Allow to cool, then add to the citrus juices in a jug.
3. Place 3–4 sponge slices in the base of a 1.1 litre (2 pint) pudding basin, spread a thinnish layer of the cheese mixture on top. Continue to layer, finishing with sponge to fit neatly on top.
4. Strain the citrus mixture, then pour very carefully over the pudding, making sure that the juices reach the bottom – this can be done by pulling back the sides with a knife. Chill to set.
5. To serve, dip the basin in hot water and invert onto the serving plate. Spread the cream evenly all over the surface. Extra cream could be piped around the base. Decorate with the chosen fruit.

LEMON CHEESE RING   Serves 6–8

This versatile dessert can be served all year round with whatever fruits are seasonal, e.g. fresh berries in the summer and oranges, grapes and pears in the Autumn. Exotic fruit such as mangoes, papaya and physallis complement the dessert any time.

45 ml (3 tbsp) water
1 sachet gelatine or 15 ml (3 tsp)
   vegetarian equivalent
395 g (14 oz) can condensed milk
250 g (9 oz) curd cheese

90 ml (6 tbsp) fresh lemon juice
5 ml (1 tsp) finely grated lemon rind
285 ml ($^1/_2$ pint) soured cream
selection of seasonal fruit

1. Place the water in a small bowl and sprinkle the gelatine on top (follow the pack instructions if using a vegetarian equivalent). Dissolve either by stirring over a pan of hot water or heating in a microwave for approximately 30 seconds on full power. Allow to cool.
2. Meanwhile whisk all the remaining ingredients, except of course the fruit, until absolutely smooth. Beat the cooled gelatine into the cheese mixture until completely incorporated.
3. Pour it into a wetted ring mould (1.1 litre, 2 pint capacity) and place in the fridge to set.
4. To serve, briefly dip the mould in hot water to loosen the sides, then invert onto the serving plate. Fill the centre with your chosen fruit and, if wished, pipe cream rosettes on top of the mousse and decorate the rosettes with small pieces of fruit.

PLUM AND ALMOND CRUMBLE

Serves 4–6

Few people can resist a hot fruit crumble. The topping for this crumble is made more interesting by adding ground almonds, which complement the plums beautifully.

735 g (1 lb 10 oz) plums,
   halved and stoned
60 ml (4 tbsp) demerara sugar
115 g (4 oz) plain flour

115 g (4 oz) ground almonds
85 g (3 oz) caster sugar
170 g (6 oz) unsalted butter

1. Pre-heat the oven to 180°C, 355°F, Gas 4. Place the plums at the bottom of a greased oven-proof dish and sprinkle the demerara sugar over.
2. Combine the flour, ground almonds and caster sugar in a large mixing bowl. Cut the butter into cubes and add to the bowl. Rub the butter into the flour mixture until it resembles breadcrumbs. Spread lightly over the fruit.
3. Bake in the oven for 30–40 mins until the crumble is golden brown.

TIRAMASU CHEESECAKE

Serves 8

Whenever I serve this dessert, I often get asked for the recipe. It combines two hugely popular puddings and is a paradise for all chocoholics. It is very rich so it is best to serve in small slices!

Base:
85 g (3 oz) butter, melted
170 g (6 oz) digestive biscuits, finely crushed
55 g (2 oz) chopped and roasted hazelnuts

Filling:
170 g (6 oz) plain chocolate
140 ml ($^{1}/_{4}$ pint) whipping cream, whipped
225 g (8 oz) mascarpone cream cheese, beaten
55 g (2 oz) caster sugar
15 ml (1 tbsp) strong black coffee, chilled

Topping:
225 g (8 oz) mascarpone cream cheese
115 g (4 oz) Greek yoghurt
8–10 chocolate-coated coffee beans
cocoa powder

1. Combine melted butter, biscuits and hazelnuts. Press into the base of a lightly-greased 18 cm (7 ins) loose-bottomed cheesecake tin, and chill.
2. While it is chilling, melt the chocolate in a bowl set over a pan of hot water and allow to cool a little. Place the mascarpone in a large bowl and fold in the coffee, sugar and chocolate, followed by the cream. Spoon into the tin and place in the fridge to chill for a few hours until set.
3. To make the topping, combine the mascarpone and yoghurt. Remove the cheesecake from the tin, and place on a serving plate. Swirl the topping over the filling and dust with sifted cocoa powder. Decorate with the beans.

BLACK AND WHITE CHOCOLATE GATEAU   Serve 8

This gâteau should appeal to all chocolate lovers! A selection of fresh berries would be an ideal accompaniment.

3 large eggs
85 g (3 oz) caster sugar
70 g (2^{1}/$_{2}$ oz) plain flour
15 g (^{1}/$_{2}$ oz) cocoa powder,
    plus extra for dusting
2.5 ml (^{1}/$_{2}$ tsp) baking powder

140 g (5 oz) white chocolate,
    broken into squares
30 g (1 oz) unsalted butter
285 ml (^{1}/$_{2}$ pint) double cream, whipped
30 ml (2 tbsp) Amaretto (optional)
55 g (2 oz) Amaretti biscuits, crushed

1. Pre-heat the oven to 180°C, 355°F, Gas 4. Grease and line 2 x 20.5 cm (8 ins) sandwich cake tins.
2. Put the eggs and sugar in a large bowl and whisk until the mixture becomes thick and pale and the whisk leaves a thick trail when lifted. Sift the flour and cocoa together and then sift over the egg mixture. Using a metal spoon, fold in the flour quickly and evenly.
3. Divide between the cake tins and spread out lightly. Bake for 20–25 mins until the cake springs back when pressed gently with the fingertips. Turn out and cool on a wire rack.
4. While the cake is in the oven, place the white chocolate in a large bowl and place over a pan of gently simmering water to melt. When it has melted, stir in the butter and continue to stir until it has melted. Allow to cool and then fold in the cream. Reserve half of this white chocolate cream and fold the Amaretti biscuits into the other half.
5. To assemble, place one sponge cake on the serving plate, sprinkle with the Amaretto, if using, and spread the Amaretti chocolate cream on top. Place the second sponge on top. Cover this with the white chocolate cream, making a swirling pattern with a fork. Dust with a little sieved cocoa powder.

ITALIAN MOCHA TRIFLE

Serves 8

A short while ago I offered to take a pudding to a friend's for a dinner party and created this trifle from my store cupboard ingredients. I am pleased to say that it was a huge success!

85 g (3 oz) sponge fingers, halved
130 g (4½ oz) Amaretti biscuits
75 ml (5 tbsp) sherry
30 ml (2 tbsp) custard powder
30 ml (2 tbsp) cocoa
10 ml (2 tsp) coffee granules

45 ml (3 tbsp) soft brown sugar
570 ml (1 pint) milk
3 bananas
285 ml (½ pint) double cream, whipped
chocolate shavings

1. Place the sponge fingers and Amaretti biscuits in the base of a large glass dish and sprinkle the sherry over.
2. Place the custard powder, cocoa, coffee and sugar in a bowl and stir in a little of the milk to form a paste. Heat the rest of the milk until it is nearly boiling and then add to the paste, stirring all the time to avoid any lumps appearing in the sauce. Return the sauce to the saucepan and bring to the boil, stirring all the time. Allow to cool.
3. Slice the bananas and arrange on top of the biscuit mixture. Pour the cooled mocha custard on top, making sure that all the bananas are covered.
4. Spread the cream on top and decorate with the chocolate curls (made by pulling a vegetable peeler along the edge of a bar of chocolate).

RHUBARB AND MERINGUE FOOL

Serves 4

This is another instant pudding which uses store cupboard ingredients. If you want to give it an extra kick, replace one of the tablespoons of orange juice with brandy.

565 g (1¼ lb) can rhubarb, drained
1 orange, finely grated zest and rind
30 ml (2 tbsp) redcurrant jelly

155 g (5½ oz) Greek yoghurt
4 meringue shells, roughly crushed

1. Place the rhubarb pieces and redcurrant jelly in a saucepan and heat gently until the jelly has melted. Remove from the heat and allow to cool. Stir in the orange rind and juice, followed by the yoghurt. Chill thoroughly.
2. Just before serving, fold in the crushed meringue and spoon into serving dishes or wine glasses.

BLACKFOREST CHEESECAKE

Serves 8

Some popular dishes from the '70s, such as the much maligned blackforest gâteau, are enjoying a revival. This is an interesting way of combining all the key ingredients.

70 g (2¹/₂ oz) butter, melted
200 g (7 oz) chocolate digestive
   biscuits, crushed
340 g (12 oz) curd cheese
30 g (1 oz) caster sugar
2 large eggs, separated
115 ml (4 fl oz) double cream,
   lightly whipped

1 sachet gelatine or 15 ml (3 tsp)
   vegetarian equivalent
140 ml (¹/₄ pint) water
115 g (4 oz) plain chocolate
   melted in a bowl over hot water
30 ml (2 tbsp) Kirsch
425 g (15 oz) can pitted cherries, drained

1. Lightly oil a 20.5 cm (8 ins) cheesecake or loose-bottomed tin. Make the base by combining the biscuits and butter and press into the tin. Chill.
2. Dissolve the gelatine in the water over a pan of hot water or by heating on full power in a microwave for 40 seconds. Allow to cool.
3. Beat the curd cheese, egg yolks, sugar and gelatine together until thoroughly combined. Slowly add the chocolate and gently fold in the cream. Whisk the egg whites until stiff and fold in one tablespoon of the whites to loosen the mixture and then fold in the remainder until the whites are no longer visible.
4. Place the cherries on the biscuit base. Sprinkle with Kirsch. Spoon the chocolate cheesecake mixture on top. Chill for several hours until set. Decorate with cream rosettes and some extra cherries or a dusting of cocoa powder.

MANGO AND RASPBERRY CHOCOLATE HEAVEN

Serves 6–8

This dessert is light and nowhere as wicked as it appears!

155 g (5¹/₂ oz) bar white chocolate,
   broken into pieces
1 large mango, peeled
   and the flesh puréed

285 ml (¹/₂ pint) whipping cream,
   whipped
510 g (1 lb 2 oz) pot natural yoghurt
250 g (9 oz) raspberries

1. Melt chocolate in a bowl over a pan of barely simmering water. Allow to cool. Combine cream, yoghurt and mango purée. Fold in the chocolate.
2. Place the raspberries in the bottom of some wine glasses or large glass bowl. Reserve a few for decoration. Spoon chocolate mixture on top and refrigerate until ready to serve. Just before serving, decorate with the reserved raspberries.

RHUBARB COMPOTE WITH MASCARPONE CREAM

Serves 6

I like to serve this dessert at the end of a fairly heavy dinner, especially in late spring when rhubarb is young and tender.

900 g (2 lb) rhubarb,
    cut into 2.5 cm (1 inch) lengths
vanilla pod
55 g (2 oz) caster sugar, or to taste

225 g (8 oz) mascarpone cheese
140 ml (¼ pint) Greek yoghurt
15 ml (1 tbsp) brandy

1. Place the rhubarb in a saucepan with the vanilla pod, sugar and a little water. Bring to the boil and then simmer very gently for a few minutes until the rhubarb is tender. Remove from the heat.
2. Remove the vanilla pod. Cut it open and scrape out the seeds into the rhubarb. Cool.
3. Cream the mascarpone cheese and fold in the yoghurt and brandy.
4. To serve, spoon the rhubarb into 6 tall glasses and spoon the cheese mixture on top.

MINI MARMALADE CHEESECAKES

Serves 6

The marmalade flavour is subtle – it adds a 'tang' to a creamy cheesecake mixture. I like to serve it surrounded by a pool of BITTER CHOCOLATE SAUCE (page 71).

250 g (9 oz) carton Ricotta cheese
30 ml (2 tbsp) caster sugar
15 ml (1 tbsp) plain flour

45 ml (3 tbsp) Seville orange marmalade
285 ml (½ pint) single cream
3 large eggs, lightly beaten

1. Pre-heat the oven to 170°C, 340°F, Gas 3–4. Grease and base line 6 ramekin dishes.
2. Place the Ricotta cheese, sugar, flour, marmalade and cream in a large mixing bowl and beat together thoroughly. Add the eggs and mix until they have been incorporated.
3. Spoon into the prepared dishes and place in a roasting dish half full of hot water and bake in the oven for 45–50 mins until the mixture is completely set (you may need to cover the cheesecakes with foil during the cooking if the tops get too brown). Remove the ramekins from the roasting tin and allow to cool.
4. To serve, run a knife around the edges and invert onto serving plates.

INDIVIDUAL BAKED 'ALASKAS'

Serves 4–6

This is an incredibly easy yet impressive dessert to serve, ideal when adults and children are dining together. In this version the ice cream is served separately and not under the meringue.

6 thick slices from
   a raspberry Swiss roll
395 g (14 oz) can peach halves, drained
2 large egg whites
pinch salt

115 g (4 oz) caster sugar
30 g (1 oz) toasted flaked almonds
340 g (12 oz) raspberries
   plus extra to serve
vanilla ice cream

1. Preheat the oven to 200°C, 390°F, Gas 6. Place the Swiss roll slices well apart on a lightly greased baking sheet. Place a few raspberries in the centre of each slice and a peach half on top, cut side down (the raspberries should fit in the peach cavity).
2. Whisk the egg whites with a pinch of salt until they are stiff. Gradually whisk in half the sugar and then fold in the rest of the sugar. Spread thickly and evenly over each portion and sprinkle with the almonds.
3. Bake in the oven for 8–10 mins until the alaskas are golden brown. Serve immediately with some raspberries and vanilla ice cream.

BLACKCURRANT FOOL

Serves 6

This is a dual purpose dessert: as well as serving it chilled, it can be frozen to make an ice cream. The alcohol in the mixture means that no beating is necessary during the freezing process – just take it out of the freezer a few minutes before serving so that it can soften a little.

340 g (12 oz) blackcurrants
115 g (4 oz) caster sugar
285 ml (½ pint) double cream

15 ml (1 tbsp) Kirsch or crème de cassis
extra sugar to taste

1. Place the blackcurrants in a saucepan with the sugar and heat VERY gently until the sugar has dissolved. Turn up the heat a little and poach the fruit until they are very soft. Allow to cool.
2. Whisk the cream with the chosen alcohol until it forms soft peaks. Sieve the blackcurrants and fold most of the purée into the cream, reserving a little for decoration. Taste to check sweetness – you may need to add a little more sugar.
3. Spoon into tall wine glasses and decorate with the reserved purée.

CHRISTMAS

STILTON AND CELERIAC SOUP
Serves 6

Stilton and celeriac are perfect partners and are delicious in this winter or Christmas soup. I like to serve it with walnut bread (most large supermarkets sell it part-baked).

30 ml (2 tbsp) sunflower oil
1 large onion, peeled and chopped
1 garlic clove, peeled and crushed
15 ml (1 tbsp) chopped fresh thyme
680 g (1½ lb) celeriac, peeled
 and cubed

140 ml (¼ pint) dry white wine
850 ml (1½ pints) good vegetable
 stock
115 g (4 oz) Stilton cheese, cubed
single cream and chopped walnuts,
 to serve

1. Gently fry the onion, garlic and thyme in the oil for 5 mins. Add the celeriac and fry for a further 5 mins. Pour in the wine and stock, bring to the boil, cover and simmer for about 20 mins until the celeriac is tender. Purée the soup so that it is completely smooth. Season with salt and black pepper.
2. Return the soup to the saucepan and stir in most of the cheese, reserving some for the garnish. Heat the soup through without boiling. Ladle into warm soup bowls, swirl with the cream and garnish with the reserved cheese and walnuts.

FESTIVE 'CRACKERS'

These crackers are absolutely delicious and bursting with flavour. Shaping the parcels into crackers will delight vegetarians at Christmas. A CRANBERRY AND PORT SAUCE (page 71), a Cumberland sauce or a rich Madeira gravy would be good accompaniment.

When using filo pastry, it is important to keep the sheets covered while preparing the crackers, as they dry out very quickly when they are exposed to the air. If you prefer, the melted butter could be replaced by about 30 ml (2 tbsp) olive oil or sunflower oil.

30 ml (2 tbsp) olive oil
1 large onion, finely chopped
2 cloves garlic, crushed
1 medium leek, sliced
1 red pepper, de-seeded and diced
115 g (4 oz) button mushrooms, sliced
70 g ($2^{1}/_{2}$ oz) Stilton, crumbled

395 g (14 oz) can artichoke hearts, drained and quartered
45 g ($1^{1}/_{2}$ oz) walnuts, roughly chopped
250 g (9 oz) pack filo pastry – should yield 18 large sheets
60 ml (4 tbsp) cranberry sauce
55 g (2 oz) butter, melted

1. Heat the oil and sauté the onion and garlic over a moderate heat for a few minutes to soften them. Add the leek, the pepper and mushrooms and fry for a few minutes until they have softened. Season with salt and fresh black pepper.
2. Remove from the heat. Stir in the Stilton, artichoke and walnuts and leave on one side until quite cool.
3. Pre-heat the oven to 190°C, 375°F, Gas 5.
4. Lay 6 sheets of pastry on the work surface and brush lightly with some butter. Continue to layer with the remaining sheets, brushing each layer with butter.
5. Spread 10 ml (2 tsp) of cranberry sauce onto each rectangle to within 5 cm (2 ins) of each of the narrow edges. Spoon on the vegetable mixture to the side nearest you, again to within 5 cm (2 ins) of the edges. Roll up away from you and pinch the end to form a cracker.
6. Brush with the remaining butter, place on a baking sheet and bake for about 20 mins until golden brown. If the cracker ends cook too quickly, cover them with pieces of foil.
7. The filling may ooze out during cooking. Don't worry if this happens; simply spoon it on the plate alongside the cracker and the chosen accompanying sauce.

STILTON AND WALNUT MOUSSE

Serves 8

These little mousses make a pretty and tasty appetiser over the Christmas period and will be enjoyed by meat-eaters and vegetarians alike. Serve with mixed salad leaves tossed in the CRANBERRY DRESSING (page 71).

30 g (1 oz) butter or margarine
30 ml (2 tbsp) plain flour
200 ml (7 fl oz) cold milk
200 ml (7 fl oz) cold vegetable stock
1 sachet gelatine or 15 ml (3 tsp)
   vegetarian equivalent
115 g (4 oz) Stilton, crumbled

2 large eggs, separated
140 ml ($^{1}/_{4}$ pint) whipping
   or double cream
55 g (2 oz) approx. walnuts,
   chopped fairly finely
paprika

1. Lightly oil and base line 8 ramekin dishes. Make a sauce by whisking the butter, flour, milk and stock together over a medium heat until it thickens and begins to boil. Remove from the heat, sprinkle over the gelatine, and whisk until dissolved. Add the cheese and stir until melted. Whisk in the egg yolks. Season with salt and fresh black pepper.
2. Whisk the cream until it forms soft peaks. Fold into the cheese mixture. Whisk the egg whites until stiff and fold gently into the mixture. Check the seasoning.
3. Spoon into the dishes, sprinkle the walnuts on top and gently stir into the mousses. Chill until set.
4. Run a knife around the edges and invert onto the serving plates. Surround with the mixed salad which has been tossed in the cranberry dressing. Sprinkle the tops of the mousses with a little paprika.

SPINACH, CRANBERRY AND RICOTTA ROULADE

Serves 6–8

I was asked by our local television station to create a starter which was healthy to eat yet suitable for a Christmas meal. This roulade is the result. It looks and tastes festive. The cranberries could be replaced with diced red peppers when not available. Serve with salad leaves tossed in a CRANBERRY DRESSING (page 71).

225 g (8 oz) frozen spinach, thawed
4 large eggs, separated
2.5 ml ($^{1}/_{2}$ tsp) freshly grated nutmeg
30 g (1 oz) fresh wholemeal
   breadcrumbs
salt and fresh ground black pepper

225 g (8 oz) Ricotta cheese
115 g (4 oz) fresh cranberries
45 ml (3 tbsp) apple juice
45 ml (3 tbsp) water
55 g (2 oz) sugar

1. Pre-heat the oven to 200°C, 390°F, Gas 6. Line a 30.5 x 20.5 cm (12 x 8 ins) Swiss roll tin with baking parchment. Cook the spinach over a gentle heat. Place spinach in a piece of muslin or clean tea towel and squeeze out the liquid. Process the spinach with the egg yolks, nutmeg, breadcrumbs and seasoning.

2. Whisk the egg whites until they are stiff. Using a metal tablespoon, fold one tablespoon of the whites into the spinach mixture and then carefully fold in the remainder.

3. Spread the mixture evenly in the prepared tin and bake in the oven for 10–15 mins until it is firm to the touch. Cover with a damp tea towel and allow to cool completely.

4. While it is cooling, dissolve the sugar in the apple juice and water in a saucepan and add the cranberries. Bring to the boil very slowly and then simmer gently for about 10 mins until the cranberries are tender but still retain their shape.

5. Invert the roulade onto a clean piece of baking parchment, remove original piece of parchment, spread with Ricotta cheese and season well. Drain the cranberries onto some kitchen paper and dot evenly over the Ricotta cheese. Trim the edges and, starting from one of the short sides, roll into a cylinder, using the parchment to help you. Cut into slices and arrange on serving plates.

MINCEMEAT AND MARZIPAN ICE CREAM   Serves 6–8

I created this ice cream after Christmas when I had some marzipan and some mincemeat left over. I was delighted with the result. It is delicious served with a dried fruit compote to which some port and orange juice has been added at the end of cooking.

115 g (4 oz) golden almond marzipan, diced
570 ml (1 pint) double cream
90 ml (6 tbsp) mincemeat
30 ml (2 tbsp) Amaretto liqueur (you could substitute brandy, rum or whisky)

1. Place the marzipan and cream in a thick-bottomed pan and stir over a gentle heat until the marzipan has dissolved. Remove from the heat and stir in the mincemeat and Amaretto. Allow to cool.

2. Pour into a plastic tub and freeze. After an hour or so, when the ice cream is beginning to freeze, remove from the freezer and stir so that all the fruit is evenly distributed. Freeze until solid.

3. Remove from the freezer 15 mins before serving to allow the ice cream time to soften slightly.

CHOCOLATE AND CHESTNUT MOUSSES

Serves 6

This is a light and interesting alternative pudding to serve at Christmas. A couple of friends who claimed not to like chestnut purée loved it – the mousse has an unusual flavour but it is difficult to identify it.

225 g (8 oz) mascarpone cream cheese
225 g (8 oz) unsweetened chestnut purée
55 g (2 oz) caster sugar
55 g (2 oz) plain chocolate drops
    or plain chocolate, chopped

2 large eggs, separated
vanilla extract, a few drops
140 ml ($^1/_4$ pint) double cream, whipped
whipped cream and grated chocolate,
    to decorate

1. Soften the mascarpone cheese in a large mixing bowl. Beat in the chestnut purée, sugar, chocolate, egg yolks and vanilla extract. Fold in the cream. Whip the egg whites until they are stiff and then fold them in very gently.
2. Spoon or pipe into tall wine glasses and decorate with the whipped cream and grated chocolate.

CHOCOLATE AND CLEMENTINE CHEESECAKE

Serves 8–10

This is a wonderful dessert to serve to chocolate lovers at Christmas time. The clementines add a seasonal flavour as well as being natural partners for chocolate. It is very rich so serve in fairly small wedges!

170 g (6 oz) chocolate digestive
    biscuits, crushed
55 g (2 oz) butter, melted
225 g (8 oz) clementines
30 g (1 oz) caster sugar
680 g (1$^1/_2$ lb) curd cheese
3 large eggs
85 g (3 oz) soft brown sugar

225 g (8 oz) plain chocolate,
    broken into squares
140 ml ($^1/_4$ pint) single cream

To decorate:
whipped cream
1 peeled clementine
sifted cocoa

1. Wash the clementines, place in a saucepan, cover with water and bring to the boil. Simmer for 25 mins until tender. Drain the clementines and purée with the caster sugar. Set aside.
2. Pre-heat the oven to 150°C, 300°F, Gas 2. Combine the biscuits and butter and spoon into a greased 20.5 cm (8 ins) cheesecake tin. Press down (a potato masher does this well) and place in the fridge to chill.

3. Beat the curd cheese, eggs and soft brown sugar together. Melt the chocolate and cream together in a bowl over a pan of gently simmering water. Allow to cool and then fold into the curd cheese mixture. Spoon over the biscuit base.
4. Put 'dollops' of the clementine purée on top of the cheesecake and swirl with a skewer or pointed knife.
5. Bake in the oven for $1^1/_4$–$1^1/_2$ hours until it is set. Allow it to cool in the switched-off oven.
6. Chill in the fridge for at least 2 hours.
7. Decorate with cream rosettes, clementine segments and a dusting of cocoa powder.

WILD MUSHROOM STRUDEL   Serves 6–8

This has to be my all-time favourite Christmas dish and everyone I have given it to has always asked for the recipe. Serve it with the PORT SAUCE *(page 69).*

85 g (3 oz) butter	10 ml (2 tsp) fresh thyme leaves
1 onion, finely chopped	55 g (2 oz) fresh white breadcrumbs
2 large cloves garlic, peeled and crushed	70 g ($2^1/_2$ oz) pine nuts, toasted
450 g (1 lb) flat mushrooms	salt and fresh ground black pepper
285 g (10 oz) chestnut mushrooms, sliced	8 large sheets filo pastry
140 g (5 oz) oyster mushrooms, sliced	85 g (3 oz) butter, melted
115 g (4 oz) button mushrooms, sliced	90 ml (6 tbsp) cranberry sauce
15 ml (1 tbsp) sherry	30 ml (2 tbsp) sesame seeds

1. Melt the butter in a large saucepan and fry the onion and garlic gently. Add the mushrooms and toss well in the garlic onions. Fry for a few more minutes.
2. Stir in the sherry, thyme, breadcrumbs, pine nuts and seasoning and remove from the heat. Allow to cool.
3. Pre-heat the oven to 200°C, 390°F, Gas 6.
4. Lay a clean tea towel onto the work surface, then lay a sheet of filo pastry on top with one of the long sides closest to you. Brush with butter, top with another sheet, repeat with two more sheets. Spread with half the cranberry sauce evenly over the pastry then spoon half the mushroom mixture along the side furthest away from you. Fold over the two shorter sides and then, using the tea towel to help you, roll the strudel towards you until all the mixture is enclosed in the pastry. Place on a large baking sheet, brush with butter and sprinkle with half the seeds. Repeat to make the second strudel.
5. Bake for 30–35 mins until the pastry is crisp and golden brown.

BBQ

FRUIT KEBABS

Serves 4–6

These are a lot of fun to make. The fruit used can be adapted according to availability and preferences. I like to serve it with a chocolate sauce to which some alcohol has been added, or you could serve it with a fruit coulis, such as raspberry.

60 ml (4 tbsp) golden syrup or maple syrup	¹/₂ small pineapple, peeled
rind and juice 1 lemon	2 bananas, peeled
30 ml (2 tbsp) sherry or dark rum	1 ripe mango, peeled
140 ml (¹/₄ pint) water	115 g (4 oz) strawberries
	115 g (4 oz) seedless red grapes

1. Place syrup, lemon rind, juice, sherry or rum and water in a shallow container. Cut fruit into bite-sized pieces. Marinate in the lemon mixture at least 2 hours.
2. Thread the fruit onto 8–12 wooden or metal skewers. Chill until ready to serve. Serve them as they are or cook them on the barbeque (perhaps glaze them with a little melted butter before placing them on the barbeque).

BAKED BANANAS

Serves 4

This wonderfully decadent treat can be baked in a medium oven for about 25 mins.

4 large firm bananas	brandy or rum
BUTTERSCOTCH SAUCE (page 68)	whipped cream or vanilla ice cream

1. Do not peel the bananas. Place them on the barbeque over a medium heat and cook until they are black all over.
2. Slice through the skin twice, 2.5cm (1 inch) apart and peel back that part of the skin. Drizzle in some brandy or rum, spoon over some butterscotch sauce and serve with scoops of ice cream.

AUBERGINE SANDWICHES

Serves 4

Slices of tomato and Mozzarella are sandwiched between slices of aubergine. They can be prepared on the barbeque in minutes or cooked in the oven in bad weather.

2 long plump aubergines
30 ml (2 tbsp) approx. olive oil
4 ripe tomatoes, each cut into 3–4 slices
250 g (9 oz) Mozzarella cheese, sliced

pesto sauce
60 ml (4 tbsp) freshly grated Parmesan
salt and fresh ground black pepper

1. Cut two slices off opposite sides of each aubergine. Set these aside to use in another dish. Slice each aubergine lengthways into 4 slices. Brush both sides with the olive oil. Cook on the barbeque (or griddle or frying pan) until golden brown and softened. Spread one side of each slice liberally with pesto sauce.
2. Place the tomato slices on top of 4 slices, top with the Mozzarella cheese and season well. Place the other slices on top with the pesto side on the inside. Sprinkle the Parmesan cheese on top. Lift carefully onto the barbeque and cook until heated through (you may wish to wrap loosely in foil).
3. OR cook in a pre-heated oven (200°C, 390°F, Gas 6) for about 15 mins until the filling has cooked and the Parmesan cheese is crisp and golden brown.

GLAMORGAN SAUSAGES

Serves 4–6

You can't beat the flavour of home-made sausages. Chill thoroughly before cooking.

1 leek, trimmed and chopped finely
½ green pepper, de-seeded
    and finely chopped
170 g (6 oz) fresh white breadcrumbs
115 g (4 oz) mature Cheddar
    or Caerphilly cheese, grated
15 ml (1 tbsp) chopped fresh parsley

10 ml (2 tsp) English mustard powder
2 large eggs, separated
a little milk
salt and fresh ground black pepper
30 ml (2 tbsp) plain flour
oil

1. Combine the first five ingredients and half the mustard in a large mixing bowl. Add the egg yolks and seasoning. If the mixture looks a little dry, add some milk, probably 30 ml (2 tbsp). Shape into sausages (you will get 8–12, depending on size) and chill for a while.
2. Whisk the egg whites a little until frothy. Combine the flour and remaining mustard powder and season. Dip the sausages in the egg white and then the flour. Brush with the oil and then cook on the barbeque, turning frequently.

GLAMORGAN SAUSAGE AND TOMATO KEBABS

Makes 8

These are very colourful, by using both red and yellow cherry tomatoes. Serve with SUN-DRIED TOMATO SAUCE *(page 70) or* ROASTED RED PEPPER SAUCE *(page 69).*

1 quantity of GLAMORGAN SAUSAGE mixture (page 65)
24 red cherry tomatoes
16 yellow cherry tomatoes
oil, preferably from a jar of sun-dried tomatoes

1. Shape the sausage mixture into 32 balls. Make up 8 kebabs, using 4 sausage balls, three red and two yellow tomatoes for each kebab. Chill until ready to cook.
2. Brush all over with the oil and cook over a moderate heat.

CHILLI BEAN AND MUSHROOM BURGERS

Serves 6

These are perfect for barbecuing – simply serve in a bap with your favourite relish. If you are not keen on spices, simply omit them. It's important to chill the burgers thoroughly before cooking so that they retain their shape.

30 ml (2 tbsp) olive oil
1 onion, peeled and finely chopped
1 small red chilli, de-seeded
   and finely chopped
1 red pepper, de-seeded
   and finely chopped
170 g (6 oz) button mushrooms,
   chopped

395 g (14 oz) can kidney beans,
   drained and rinsed
45 g (1½ oz) chopped mixed nuts
115 g (4 oz) fresh breadcrumbs
30 ml (2 tbsp) mango chutney
1 egg yolk
salt and fresh ground black pepper
plain flour

1. Gently fry the onion, chilli and pepper in the oil for a few minutes until they have softened. Add the mushrooms and cook for a few more minutes. Transfer to a blender or liquidiser together with the kidney beans and blend briefly – you need to retain some texture.
2. Transfer to a mixing bowl and stir in the nuts, breadcrumbs, chutney, egg yolk, salt and pepper until they are all combined. Cover and place in the fridge to chill completely. Shape into 6 burgers and then coat in the flour.
3. Use a fish slice or spatula to carefully place them on the barbeque and cook for 10–15 mins until they are cooked and the surfaces are crispy (you will need to turn them often to prevent them from sticking).

SAUCES

MUSHROOM AND WHITE WINE SAUCE

Serves 6

It is well worth the expense of using the dried porcini mushrooms in this sauce as they really bring out the flavour of the mushrooms.

10 g (^{1}/$_{4}$ oz) dried porcini mushrooms
225 ml (8 fl oz) warm water
30 g (1 oz) butter
1 onion, peeled and very finely chopped
2 garlic cloves, peeled and crushed
225 g (8 oz) chestnut mushrooms, sliced

315 ml (11 fl oz) good vegetable stock
315 ml (11 fl oz) dry white wine
15 ml (1 tbsp) cornflour
100 ml (3^{1}/$_{2}$ fl oz) crème fraiche
salt and fresh ground black pepper

1. Place the porcini mushrooms in a bowl, pour over the warm water and leave to soak for 20–30 mins. Drain, reserving the liquid and chop the mushrooms.
2. Melt the butter in a saucepan and fry the onion and garlic over a gentle heat for a few minutes until the onion is soft. Add the chestnut mushrooms, stir well to coat them in the buttery onions and fry for a few minutes further until they are cooked. Pour in the reserved mushrooms, mushroom liquid, the stock and white wine, bring to the boil and cook for 10–15 mins until the liquid has reduced by a half. Blend the cornflour with a little cold water and add to the sauce. Bring to the boil, stirring continuously, and then simmer for a couple of minutes. Add the crème fraiche and seasoning and heat through.

PESTO SAUCE

Pesto sauce adds so much flavour to so many dishes: an interesting alternative to garlic butter; stir into tomato-based sauces; add a spoonful to a jacket potato etc. Jars are readily available but the flavour of home-made pesto sauce is far superior.

55 g (2 oz) fresh basil leaves	115 ml (4 fl oz) extra virgin olive oil
30 g (1 oz) pine nuts	55 g (2 oz) fresh grated Parmesan cheese
2 cloves garlic, peeled and chopped	salt and fresh ground black pepper

1. Place the basil, pine nuts, garlic and olive oil in a blender or food processor and blend until smooth and all the ingredients are well blended.
2. Spoon into a bowl and mix in the Parmesan cheese. Season to taste.

MEXICAN CHILLI SAUCE

Serves 6

30 ml (2 tbsp) olive oil	2 fresh chillies, de-seeded and chopped
1 medium onion, chopped	$1^1/_2$ x 395 g (14 oz) tins chopped tomatoes
2 cloves garlic, peeled and chopped	140 ml ($^1/_4$ pint) water
5 ml (1 tsp) ground cumin	30 ml (2 tbsp) tomato purée
2.5 ml ($^1/_2$ tsp) ground coriander	salt and fresh ground black pepper

1. Heat the oil in a saucepan and fry the onion and garlic until soft. Add the spices and chillies and cook briefly.
2. Add the tomatoes, water and purée and season. Bring to the boil and simmer gently for about an hour.
3. Liquidise the sauce until it is nearly smooth but still has some texture.

BUTTERSCOTCH SAUCE

For those with a sweet tooth, this sauce is just wonderful. It keeps well in the fridge and freezes very well.

55 g (2 oz) butter
115 g (4 oz) demerara sugar
140 ml ($^1/_4$ pint) double cream

Place all the ingredients in a small pan and heat together gently, stirring until the butter and sugar have dissolved and you have a smooth glossy sauce.

PORT SAUCE

This is a natural partner for the WILD MUSHROOM STRUDEL (page 63). I often make double the quantity because it is so popular.

1 small onion, chopped finely
30 g (1 oz) butter
30 ml (2 tbsp) plain flour
710 ml (1¼ pints) good
   vegetable stock
salt and fresh ground black pepper

small sprig each of fresh thyme
   and parsley
2 bay leaves
15 ml (1 tbsp) tomato purée
30 ml (2 tbsp) port

1. Melt the butter in a saucepan and fry the onion for a few minutes until golden brown. Stir in the flour and cook until it browns then remove it from the heat. Stir in the vegetable stock. Return to the heat and bring to the boil, stirring to prevent any lumps forming. Add the herbs, tomato purée and seasoning and boil for a while until the liquid has reduced to about 425 ml (¾ pint).
2. Strain the sauce into a clean saucepan, discarding the onion and herbs, then add the port. Bring to the boil and simmer for 2 mins. Check the seasoning.

ROASTED RED PEPPER SAUCE

Serves approx. 6–8

This is a colourful sauce and so full of flavour. It goes with a variety of dishes, particularly those which include aubergines, courgettes and mushrooms.

2 large, red peppers, quartered
   and de-seeded
1 shallot, peeled and chopped
1 clove garlic, peeled and chopped
15 ml (1 tbsp) olive oil

4 ripe tomatoes, skinned, de-seeded
   and diced
115 ml (4 fl oz) vegetable stock
salt and fresh ground black pepper
30 g (1 oz) unsalted butter

1. Place the peppers under a hot grill and cook until the skins are black and blistered. Place in a plastic bag and leave to cool.
2. Meanwhile, fry the shallot and garlic gently in the oil until the onion has softened. Add the tomatoes and cook for a couple of minutes.
3. Skin and chop the peppers and add to the pan with the stock. Bring to the boil, season and then simmer for a few minutes. Liquidise and, if wished, pass through a sieve. Return to the pan and stir in the butter, to give the sauce a glossy finish and a touch of richness.

AVOCADO SALSA

2 ripe avocado pears, diced
4 spring onions, finely sliced
30 ml (2 tbsp) fresh lime juice

30 ml (2 tbsp) fresh coriander
salt and fresh ground black pepper

Combine all the ingredients and chill for about half an hour.

HARISSA

This is a spicy North African–Moroccan paste. It can be bought ready made in the supermarket but not many stores stock it. It is very easy to make and the flavour of the home-made version is far superior. This recipe is based on Delia Smith's.

115 ml (4 fl oz) extra virgin olive oil
7.5 ml (1½ tsp) cayenne pepper
30 ml (2 tbsp) ground cumin
30 ml (2 tbsp) sun-dried tomato purée

1 lemon, juice only
4 sun-dried tomatoes,
    very finely chopped

Combine all the ingredients, except the sun-dried tomatoes, in a bowl and whisk together until they are well blended and then stir in the sun-dried tomatoes.

SUN-DRIED TOMATO SAUCE

30 ml (2 tbsp) olive oil (preferably from the sun-dried tomatoes jar)
1 small onion, finely chopped
1 clove garlic, chopped
395 g (14 oz) can chopped tomatoes
4 sun-dried tomatoes which have been reconstituted in oil
10 ml (2 tsp) balsamic vinegar
140 ml (¼ pint) approx. light vegetable stock

1. Fry the onion and garlic in the oil over a moderate heat until soft. Add the tomatoes, bring to the boil and reduce the heat so that the sauce simmers gently. Season with salt and pepper. Cook, uncovered, for about 15 mins.
2. Thinly slice the sun-dried tomatoes and add to the sauce. Pour the mixture into a blender or food processor and blend to a purée. Add sufficient stock to reach the required consistency.
3. Add the vinegar and check the seasoning.

BITTER CHOCOLATE SAUCE

200 g (7 oz) good quality plain chocolate
30 ml (2 tbsp) brandy
60 ml (4 tbsp) double cream
1 small cup strong black coffee, chilled

Put chocolate, brandy, cream and half the coffee in a saucepan. Heat gently to melt the chocolate. Add more coffee to achieve the desired taste and/or consistency.

RASPBERRY COULIS

225 g (8 oz) fresh raspberries
    (if frozen, thaw and drain)

15–30 ml (1–2 tbsp sugar), to taste
Kirsch, to taste

1. Put the raspberries in a blender or food processor and blend to a purée.
2. Pass the purée through a nylon sieve, then stir in the sugar and Kirsch.

CRANBERRY DRESSING

60 ml (4 tbsp) cranberry sauce
45 ml (3 tbsp) olive oil
90 ml (6 tbsp) apple juice

30 ml (2 tbsp) red wine vinegar
5 ml (1 tsp) wholegrain mustard
salt and pepper

Put all ingredients in a screw-top jar. Shake until well blended. Check seasoning

CRANBERRY AND PORT SAUCE

450 g (1 lb) cranberries
90 ml (6 tbsp) red wine
45 ml (3 tbsp) fresh orange juice
85 g (3 oz) sugar

10 ml (2 tsp) arrowroot, dissolved
    in 30 ml (2 tbsp) water
60 ml (4 tbsp) redcurrant jelly
60 ml (4 tbsp) port
140 ml ($^1/_4$ pint) single cream

1. Place the cranberries, orange juice, wine and sugar in a saucepan. Bring to the boil and simmer for 3–4 mins until the cranberries are tender.
2. Stir in the arrowroot and jelly and cook until thickened. Add the port and cream. Taste and add more sugar, if needed.

INGREDIENTS INDEX

INGREDIENTS INDEX

INGREDIENTS INDEX

INGREDIENTS INDEX

INGREDIENTS INDEX

INGREDIENTS INDEX

INGREDIENTS INDEX

ABOUT THE WI

If you have enjoyed this book, the chances are that you would enjoy belonging to the largest women's organisation in the country – the National Federation of Women's Institutes, or the WI as it is usually known.

We are friendly, go-ahead, like-minded women, who derive enormous satisfaction from all the movement has to offer. The list is long – you can make new friends, have fun and companionship, visit new places, develop new skills, take part in community services, fight local campaigns, become a WI Market producer, and play an active role in an organisation that has a national voice.

The WI is the only women's organisation in the country that owns an adult education establishment. At Denman College, you can take a course in anything from car maintenance to paper sculpture, from book binding to yoga, or cordon bleu cookery to fly fishing.

For more information, write to the **National Federation of Women's Institutes, 104 New Kings Road, London SW6 4LY, phone 0171-371-9300. The NFWI Wales Office is at 19 Cathedral Road, Cardiff CF1 9LJ, phone 01222-221712. For more information and a catalogue about WI Books, contact WI Books, Glebe House, Church Street, Crediton, Devon EX17 2AF, phone 01363 777575.**

ABOUT THE AUTHOR

Sîan Cook is married with two young children. She was born and brought up in Wales. After gaining a B.Sc. Hons in Hotel and Catering Administration at the University of Surrey, she joined Cadbury Schweppes as a graduate and progressed to National Account Manager. Subsequently she operated a chain of coffee shops for Perrings Stores in the South of England.

After her first baby, she gave up work briefly and then retrained. She completed a Teacher Training course, specialising in teaching cookery.

Sîan is a self-taught cook for whom cookery has always been both a passion and a hobby. She became a vegetarian 15 years ago but continued to eat fish for a while. She has already had recipes published in two cookbooks, *The Food Aid Book* and *Fit for a Princess*, and now teaches Adult Studies at Newbury College and is a cookery tutor at Denman College.

MORE FROM WI BOOKS

There are lots more books on cookery and crafts available from WI Books, the WI's own publishing company. WI Books publishes and makes available books of good value and special interest to WI members. There are many titles on Cooking, Crafts and Gardening, Painting and Drawing, as well as histories of the WI and of Denman College. A catalogue is available from WI Books, Glebe House, Church Street, Crediton, Devon EX17 2AF.

Prices for 1999 are shown for the following cookery titles selected from the list, and written by WI Members. These titles are also available to the general public. Contact WI Books at the address above or the distributor, Biblios, Star Road, Partridge Green, West Sussex RH13 8LD.

The new "WI Book of ... " cookery series, tried and tested by WI Members:

Bread and Bakes	*Kay Bradley*	£4.95
Cakes	*Jill Brand*	£4.95
Cooking for One	*Margaret Foss*	£4.95
Jams and Preserves	*Pat Hesketh*	£4.95
Salsas and Unusual Preserves	*Grace Mulligan*	£4.95
Sweets and Chocolates	*Clift, Green & Phillips*	£4.95

Other titles available in the original series, tried and tested by WI Members:

Biscuits	£3.95	**Pastry**	£1.80
Fish and Seafood	£2.95	**Soups and Starters**	£2.95
Microwave Cookery	£2.95	**Vegetables and Salads**	£2.95

A Taste of WI Markets   *by WI Market Members*   £4.95
More than 135 recipes celebrate WI Markets' outstanding reputation as a source of fresh homemade cooking.

The Family Vegetarian   *by Mary Norwak*   £4.95
An extensive variety of delicious non-meat dishes with nutrition advice. For the family who want vegetarian meals within everyday cooking.

Simply Good Food   *by NFWI Wales*   £4.95
Over 130 recipes to make you feel well, look well and be well, using foods low in fat, salt and sugar, and high in fibre, to produce delicious and healthy food.